THE
ELEMENTS OF MUSIC

by

REGINALD HUNT

D.Mus. London, F.R.C.O., F.L.C.M.

Director
London College of Music

A

E. A. L?ᵈ
12/. NETT

First Published 1959

Printed in Great Britain by
Lowe & Brydone (Printers) Limited, London N.W.10

FOREWORD

This book is intended in the first place for use in connection with the theoretical examinations of the London College of Music, the material being presented as far as possible in the same order as that followed in the published examination syllabus, except that melody writing, harmony, free counterpoint and history of music are outside the scope of a work of this nature. It is also recommended for general use.

Published under the authority of the Executive Council of the London College of Music

CONTENTS

MUSICAL SOUNDS – THEIR PITCH – NOTATION – POSITION ON THE KEYBOARD – CLEFS – POSITION OF NOTES ON THE STAFF OR STAVE – LEGER LINES

Musical Sounds

1. Sounds in music are represented by signs, which not only indicate their highness or lowness (their height or depth), i.e. their **pitch**,* but their **duration** or **length** as well.

The System of Naming Musical Sounds

2. The pitch of musical sounds is indicated by letters of the alphabet. Although musical sounds cover a wide range, seven letters only are used— A B C D E F G—over and over again.   Thus there is an A as the bottom note of most pianos, other A's at regular intervals and an A at the top or very near the top, thus:—

---

* *This footnote provides information which may be left to a much later stage.*

The pitch of a sound depends upon the number of *vibrations* (i.e. the rapid motion of the string of a piano or other instrument forward and backward) required to produce it.   The greater the speed, or the *frequency*, of the vibrations the higher the pitch.   The vibration of the string or strings (or of the column of air in a wind instrument) is communicated to the air in the form of *sound waves* which reach the listener's ear.   From the ear a message is transmitted to the brain which interprets the message as *sound*.

The sound called Middle C on the pianoforte is produced by 256 vibrations a second: the next note C, higher on the keyboard, is produced by double the number of vibrations, viz. 528.

Musical sounds are produced by *regular* vibrations.   If the vibrations are *not regular, noise* is the result.

The degree of loudness of a sound is called its *intensity*.   The intensity of a sound depends upon the size or *amplitude* of the vibrations (i.e. the distance the string is displaced each way from its position at rest).

The quality of sound is called its *timbre*.   (For instance, contrast the timbre of a violin with that of a trumpet.)

If all the A's were sounded together they would give the impression of one big composite note, there being no disagreeable clash: similarly all the B's would sound like one big note.   Thus the letters repeat themselves every 8th note.   The prefix " oct " means 8, as in " octagon " (an eight-sided figure).   Each new A, B, C, etc. is said then to be an **octave** (or eight notes) higher than the preceding (lower) A, B, C, etc.

Musical Notation

3.   Musical signs denoting pitch are called **notes**, and the method by which sounds are shown on paper is called **musical notation.**   For this an arrangement of five lines and four spaces called the **staff** or **stave** is used.   Though there is no hard or fast rule, the word " staff " is more often used as an *adjective* (e.g. " staff notation "—or showing notes on five lines and four spaces) and " stave " as a *noun* (e.g. " notes on the stave ").

Keys

4.   The wooden levers—white and black—on the pianoforte, which we push down or depress, are called **keys**, and they are known by the names of the notes whose sounds they give.   Thus, if after having read the note A on the stave, we depress the key for A, we produce the A sound. The whole series of keys on the pianoforte is described as the **keyboard.** It must be added that the word " key " has also a totally different meaning (See paragraph 63).

Clefs

5.   The stave means nothing to us musically unless we know " which notes are which " upon it.   To fix the position of the notes on the stave a sign called a **clef** is used.   For the right-hand (upper half) of the keyboard the **G clef or treble clef** is used:—

Though there is now little resemblance, this sign was once the letter G. Until the clef is added there is nothing to show the position of the notes on the stave.   The middle curl of the G clef fixes the note G as on the second line counting upwards:—

Any line could have been chosen for G, but custom has fixed on the second line up.   G having been fixed, the other notes fall into their places, *both lines and spaces being utilised.*

The following arrangement shows the naming of the lines and spaces separately, and makes memorisation easy.   The names of the notes in

2

the spaces spell FACE, and the doggerel sentence " Every Good Boy Deserves Favour " will be a good memory-aid for the lines.

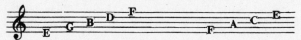

The Bass Clef

6. For the left-hand (lower half) of the keyboard, the F line is fixed by the **F clef or bass clef.** Two forms are met with:—

The second one is really the correct way. The sign is supposed to be a corruption of the shape of the letter F (*F* or *ʒ*) and the *two dots* are most important as they *enclose the F line*:—

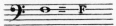

The other notes fall into their places, both lines and spaces being utilised:—

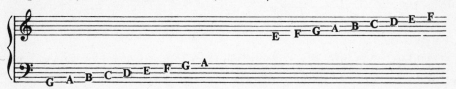

Memory-aids this time are " Good Boys Deserve Favour Always " and " All Cows Eat Grass."

Both Staves Bracketed

7. In piano music the two staves are put together, being joined together by a line and a bracket (or brace) thus:—

It will be noticed that there is a gap between the top note A of the bass stave and the bottom note E on the treble stave, B, C and D being the missing notes.

We therefore put a B resting on top of the bass stave, and " hang " a D underneath the treble stave. This time the letter names are shown as musical notes. These notes are explained later in paragraph 13 as **semibreves.**

3

This leaves out the note C, the middle note of the keyboard. We therefore have recourse to what is called a **leger line.** The word "leger" is really the same as the word "ledger" (account book). Such a book has many lines.

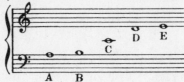

Note: Both staves could be used as above, with a continuous middle line for middle C, making eleven lines in all. Such an arrangement is known as the **great stave** in musical theory. It is never used in practical music because it confuses and tires the eye: the blank space between the treble and bass staves is a most necessary convenience occupied only by occasional short leger lines.

Leger Lines

8. As indicated above, these are short horizontal lines added above or below the staves when the notes go too high or too low to be shown on the staves themselves. **Middle C** can be shown either on a leger line above the bass stave or on a leger line below the treble stave, the same note being sounded in each case:—

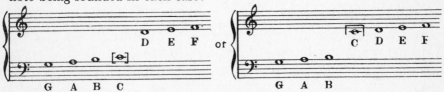

Middle C is *not* written exactly midway between the two staves, but as a note attached either to the bass or to the treble stave.

The higher notes of the bass are often written as belonging to the treble stave, and the lower notes of the treble as belonging to the bass stave, by means of the use of leger lines:—

The above examples represent exactly the same sounds.

Leger Lines and the Limitations of the Stave

9. The notes on the pianoforte keyboard, including one leger line below the bass stave and one leger line above the treble stave, appear as follows:—

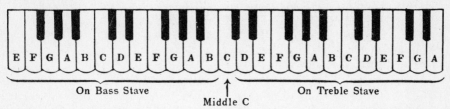

The above diagram shows less than half of the extent of the keyboard, which normally has at least 52 white notes instead of the 25 shown: hence the need for more leger lines than one above or below.

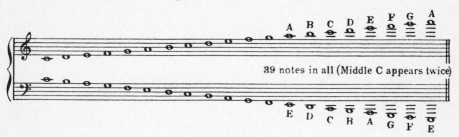

Too Many Leger Lines confuse the Eye

10. If higher or lower notes required the use of more than four leger lines as used in the above example the reader's eye would be confused. For very high notes, therefore, it is customary to write the notes which produce sounds an octave below those required, and to put the direction "8ve . . ." or simply "8 . . ." above the passage. The Italian term is "ottava"—abbreviated to "8va."

Instead of laboriously writing

—we write the signs for B, C, D an octave lower, put "8ve . . ." above them, and the required high notes will be played.

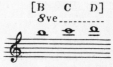

Similarly, instead of writing

—we write the signs for E, D, C an octave higher, put "8ve . . ." below them, and the required low notes will be played.

Sometimes the Italian word **bassa** is put with " 8va " thus **8va bassa,** the effect being the same as in the last example above.

The figure **8** *below each note* of a series of bass notes means that each is to be played *with* its octave below:—

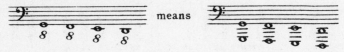

The direction is sometimes " con 8 " (" with 8 ").

Loco

11. After the " 8ve . . . " direction the word **loco** may be used to indicate a return to the proper pitch of the notes. It is an Italian word meaning " in its proper place." The English words " local," " locality " and " location " come to mind in this connection.

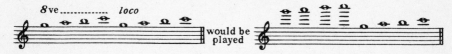

" Loco " is not much used now. The cessation of the line of dots following " 8ve " is sufficient indication of the resumption of proper pitch:—

QUESTIONS AND EXERCISES ON CHAPTER I

1. (a) How are the black notes grouped on the piano keyboard?

   (b) With the help of the keyboard diagram (paragraph 2) and using the black-note grouping as a guidance, sound the following white notes:—
      (i) all the F's (to the left of each group of three black notes);
      (ii) all the B's (to the right of each group of three black notes);
      (iii) all the D's (lying between each group of two black notes).

   (c) Locate the other four white notes in similar fashion.

   (d) Press down the sustaining (right foot) pedal, keep it down, then play all the A's, letting them all sound together as " one big composite note."

   (e) Release the pedal to stop the sound, then depress it again, keep it down then play all the B's, letting them all sound together.

   (f) Treat C, D, E, F and G similarly.

2. (a) Could you name these notes?

   (b) If not, why not?

   (c) Add the necessary sign to make the above four notes read as FADC.

6

(d) Add the necessary sign to make the above four notes read as ACFE.

3. Name these notes:—

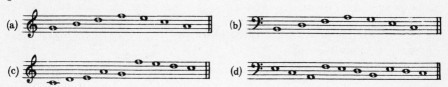

(a) (b)

(c) (d)

4. Write these notes in groups of two, one note in each two-group at an octave distance from the other. Separate each group from the next by what is called a **double bar line** thus:—

Bars and bar lines are explained in Chapter III.

These are the notes to be written:—

Treble Clef — Middle C, C above; DD; EE; GG; AA; BB.

Bass Clef — Middle C, C below; BB; AA; GG; FF; EE.

5. Practise drawing G and F clefs, taking care with the curl round the second line up in the G clef, and adding the two dots to the F clef to enclose the F line (fourth up).

6. Using leger lines where necessary, write on the treble stave the following notes:—
A in a space; *B in a space; C in a space; F in a space; E on a line; F on a line; G on a line; A on a line.

7. Similarly write these notes on the bass stave;—
G in a space; A in a space; E in a space; *B in a space; F on a line; C on a line; D on a line; A on a line; E on a line.

* N.B.—If a note is above or below a leger line, it is really in a *space* between that leger line and the next leger line, though the latter is not shown; and if a note is resting on top of a stave or hanging below it, it is really in a space between the top or bottom line of the stave and the first leger line (though, again, the leger line is not shown).

8. (a) Name these notes:—

(b) Write them with the direction " 8ve . . . " so as to make them more easily read.

9. (a) Name these notes:—

(b) Write them with the direction " 8ve . . . " so as to make them more easily read.

10. Re-write the following, using " 8ve . . . " and " loco " as required:—

11. Re-write the following, using " 8va bassa . . . " and " loco " as required:—

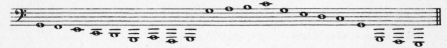

12. Write the following on the treble stave, to sound one octave higher:—

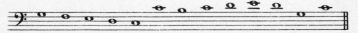

13. Write the notes in No. 12 on the treble stave to sound two octaves higher.

14. Write the following on the bass stave to sound one octave lower.

15. Write the notes in No. 14 on the bass stave to sound two octaves lower.

N.B.—For Questions 16 and 17 the relative position of middle C on (a) the treble stave, and (b) the bass stave should be clearly understood:—

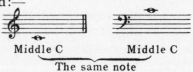

Middle C   Middle C
The same note

16. Re-write the following *at the same pitch* on the bass stave:—

17. Re-write the following *at the same pitch* on the treble stave:—

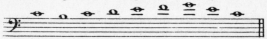

CHAPTER II

THE DURATION OR LENGTH OF SOUNDS

12. In paragraph 1 it was stated that musical sounds are represented by signs (viz., notes) which not only indicate their **pitch** (highness or lowness) but also their **duration** or **length**.

13. The longest note in common use is the **semibreve**, written:—

To write this do not try to draw a careful ellipse, but draw an upper and a lower curve, joined at each end:—

The word means literally " half-short," the choice of this unsuitable name for the *longest* note being explained by the fact that, of the various notes in use up to about the end of the fifteenth century, only the *shortest* has been retained for general use, to become the longest in modern times.

The **breve** (or " short "), written:—   is, however,

still to be met with in church and organ music. It is twice the length of the semibreve.

14. The other notes are now to be given. In each case each succeeding note is half the length of its predecessor.

(a) The **minim**, written:—   or   is an " open "

note like the semibreve, but with a vertical line attached. The open, curved part is known as the **head**, and the line is known as the **stem.**

When the head of the note is in the *upper* half of the stave, the stem begins on the *left* side of the head and goes *downward*. When the head is in the *lower* half of the stave, the stem begins on the *right* side of the head and goes *upward*. When the head is on the *middle* line of the stave the stem may be on the right *or* left side, and up *or* down:—

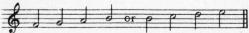

This is the universal rule for all notes with stems, and a manuscript which disregards it looks odd to the educated musician.

The rule is broken, however, when it becomes necessary to distinguish between the different parts or voices which share the same stave, as for instance in a hymn tune:—

Treble – upward stem
Alto – downward stem

Tenor – upward stem
Bass – downward stem

There are **two minims in one semibreve**: that is, one semibreve equals in duration two minims.

(b) The **crotchet**, written:— or is, like the minim, a note with a stem but has the head " filled in."
While semibreve and minim may be called *white* notes, the crotchet is a *black* note, and all the others still to be described are black also.
There are **two crotchets in one minim**: that is, one minim equals in duration two crotchets.

(c) The **quaver**, written:— or is like the crotchet, but with a " hook " attached to its stem.
There are **two quavers in one crotchet**: that is, one crotchet equals in duration two quavers.

(d) The **semiquaver**, written:— or has two hooks and is half the length of the quaver.

(e) The **demi semiquaver**, written:— or has three hooks and is half the length of the semiquaver.

(f) There is an even shorter note, the **hemi demi semiquaver**, written:— or which has four hooks, and which is half the length of the demi semiquaver, but its use is much rarer than that of the others.

10

15. The relation of the various notes is shown in the following table:—

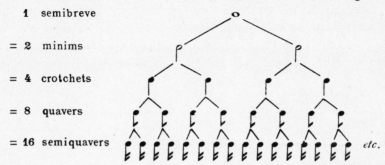

1	semibreve
= 2	minims
= 4	crotchets
= 8	quavers
= 16	semiquavers

This relation of the other notes to the semibreves is very important. [1 semibreve = 2 minims = 4 crotchets = 8 quavers = 16 semiquavers = 32 demisemiquavers]. These numbers, 1, 2, 4, 8, 16 and 32 will be referred to in Chapter III.

Note: As an exercise in simple arithmetic the relation of the other notes to each other may be worked out: e.g. How many quavers in a minim? How many semiquavers in a crotchet?

16. Notes with hooks (quavers and shorter notes) may have their hooks joined:—

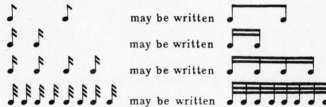

17. There is another system of naming notes instead of calling them semibreves, minims, etc., this utilises the relation of them all to the semibreve, thus:—

o	the	whole	note			
♩	the	half	note	(because	half	of a semibreve)
♩	the	quarter	note	(because	quarter	of a semibreve)
♪	the	eighth	note	(because	eighth	of a semibreve)
♬	the	sixteenth	note	(because	sixteenth	of a semibreve)
♬	the thirtysecondth note			(because thirtysecondth of a semibreve)		

This system is used in Germany and America, but it is not recommended. Simple (primary) music very largely makes use of the **crotchet** as the **"one-beat"** note (See Chapter III). To call the note that so often stands for one full beat by the name "quarter note" is liable to cause confusion.

11

18. Notes may be joined together by a **tie** or **bind** (See also paragraph 41).

A *tie* or *bind* is a curved line joining the *heads* (not the stems) of notes:—

 This means that the first note is played and then held on through the duration of the second note, *which is not sounded separately*.

 These would sound the same as

Note: To avoid confusion later it must be explained that the *curved line* in music is used in more than one way.

It is called a *tie* or *bind* when it joins *notes of the same pitch*, as above. For other uses of the curved line See Chapter IV, paragraph 41, and Chapter XII, paragraph 192, 193.

QUESTIONS AND EXERCISES ON CHAPTER II

1. What do musical notes indicate in addition to showing the pitch of sounds?

2. (a) What is the longest note now in common use?
   (b) What is unusual about its name?
   (c) What note longer than that referred in 2 (a) is still to be met with?

3. Write the names of the different kinds of notes, beginning with the longest and continuing until the shortest is reached.

4. On the treble stave write the following pairs of notes (at different pitches), one of each pair having an upturned stem and the other a downturned stem.* Leger lines may be used as required. Separate each pair from the next pair by means of a double bar-line (See Question 4 following Chapter I, for an example of a double bar-line).
   (a) CC as semibreves; (b) DD as minims; (c) EE as crotchets; (d) FF as quavers; (e) GG as semiquavers; (f) AA as demisemiquavers.
   Do not join the hooks.

5. Write in the same way the corresponding notes on the bass stave.

6. Write the following groups of notes, joining their hooks as straight lines:—

   Treble stave: (a) Four quavers—note A.
   　　　　　　　(b) Four semiquavers—note G.
   　　　　　　　(c) Eight demisemiquavers—note F.
   　　　　　　　(d) Eight hemidemisemiquavers—note E.
   Bass stave:　Similarly.

*Except in the case of semibreves.

12

7. (a) On the treble stave write eight semiquavers joined together by their hooks as straight lines: connect their heads by ties and name the note whose duration they equal when considered as one long sound.

   (b) On the bass stave write eight quavers with their hooks joined: connect their heads by ties and name the long note whose duration they equal.

8. How many semiquavers   are there in a semibreve?
               semiquavers   are there in a minim?
               semiquavers   are there in a crotchet?
               semiquavers   are there in a quaver?
               quavers   are there in a semibreve?
               quavers   are there in a minim?
               quavers   are there in a crotchet?
               demisemiquavers are there in a semibreve?
               demisemiquavers are there in a minim?
               demisemiquavers are there in a crotchet?
               demisemiquavers are there in a quaver?

9. What name is given in America to the crotchet? minim? semibreve? semiquaver?

10. Give two names for each of these notes:—

    𝅗𝅥 : ♪ : 𝅝 : 𝅘𝅥 : ♪ : 𝅘𝅥𝅯 : 𝅘𝅥𝅰 :

11. (a) What is a " tie " or " bind "?
    (b) What is its effect?
    (c) Write an example of a tie and describe its effect.

12. Write examples of one note equal in duration to (a) four crotchets; (b) four quavers; (c) four semiquavers; (d) four demisemiquavers; (e) two semiquavers; (f) two quavers; (g) two crotchets.

CHAPTER III

TIME – TIME SIGNATURES – SIMPLE TIME – RHYTHM AND RHYTHMIC PATTERN

19. Sounds are grouped by **accent** (which means stress, emphasis or force) into sets called **bars**, the **bar-line** being the conventional sign to show where the accent comes.

In language (verse) accented syllables are marked thus:— —

unaccented syllables are marked thus:— ∪

Example: Once in roy - al Da - vid's ci - ty.

In the above line the accented syllables occur at regular intervals, every other syllable being accented.

In music this sign:— > is used to indicate accent. If we put crotchets to each syllable, this would be the result:—

Once in roy - al Da - vid's ci - ty.

Instead, however, of putting in these accent marks, the musical procedure is to put a vertical line before each accented note. The above then would appear thus:—

The vertical lines are **bar-lines** and the spaces or sets or compartments between are called **bars**. These bar-lines *do not break up or divide the music*, which goes on continuously, the last note of one bar pressing forward into the next bar, thus:—

This grouping into bars is what is known as TIME.

> N.B.—*Time* has other meanings also; it may refer to the *speed* or *pace* of the music (quick time, moderate time, slow time) and it may refer to the *duration* or *length* of notes as shown in Chapter II.

20. The crotchets in paragraph 19 represent a regular and even **pulse** or **beat,** alternately strong and weak as in marching LEFT-right LEFT-right.

This time would be called **Two beats in a bar** or **Duple Time.**

—" *Duple* " means *two* : as in *du*et (music for Two performers)—

— *du*el (combat for Two opponents)—

21. When the strong pulse or beat occurs on every *third* beat, the music groups itself into threes:—

       –   ᴗ   ᴗ   –   ᴗ   ᴗ   –   ᴗ   ᴗ   –
What's this dull town to   me? Ro-bin's not   here

| ♩ ♩ ♩ | ♩ ♩ ♩ | ♩ ♩ ♩ | ♩ *etc.*

Three beats in a bar or Triple Time.

— " *Tri*-ple " means *three*: as in *tri*-angle (three-sided figure)   —
—   *tri*-cycle (three-wheeled cycle) —

22. When the strong pulse occurs on every *fourth* beat, the music groups itself into fours, but in this case a *medium* accent is given to the third beat in the bar:—

    – ᴗ ᴗ ᴗ   – ᴗ ᴗ ᴗ   – ᴗ ᴗ ᴗ   – ᴗ ᴗ ᴗ
Men of Har-lech, on to   glo-ry! See your ban-ners, famed in   sto- ry

| ♩ ♩ ♩ ♩ | ♩ ♩ ♩ ♩ | ♩ ♩ ♩ ♩ | ♩ ♩ ♩ ♩

Four beats in a bar or Quadruple Time.

— Compare:—   *quad*-rangle (four-sided court)   —
—   *quad*-ruped (four-footed animal) —

N.B.—When a piece of music begins on the first beat of the bar, it is customary to omit the first bar-line,

thus:—

23. **The Double Bar-line** marks the end of a piece of music or the end of an important section. It may occur anywhere in a bar and does not necessarily come before an accented beat. (See Question 4 following Chaper I.)

24   **The Time Signature.** The time (number of beats in the bar) is always indicated at the beginning of a piece of music, and this indication or sign is called the **time signature**.

The most sensible type of time signature would be as follows:—

2 crotchets in a bar:— $\frac{2}{\text{♩}}$

3 crotchets in a bar:— $\frac{3}{\text{♩}}$

4 crotchets in a bar:— $\frac{4}{\text{♩}}$

3 minims in a bar:— $\frac{3}{\text{𝅗𝅥}}$

4 quavers in a bar:— $\frac{4}{\text{♪}}$
and so on.

Any kind of note can be chosen as the " one-beat note," but it is very rare to use the longest (semibreve) or any note shorter than a semiquaver.

25. Time signatures are, however, not shown in this way. The upper figure showing the *number* of beats in the bar is retained, but, instead of the actual " one-beat note " appearing underneath the number on top, *another figure* represents the " one-beat note " or time unit.

Paragraph 15 shows *the relation of all notes to the semibreve.* The numbers on the left in the diagram in that paragraph are used to represent their respective notes in the time signatures.

Because there are 2 minims in a semibreve—
the time signature for 2 minims in a bar is . $\frac{2}{2}$ – *not* $\frac{2}{\rho}$

For 3 minims in a bar—
the time signature is . . . . $\frac{3}{2}$ – *not* $\frac{3}{\rho}$

Because there are 4 crotchets in a semibreve—
the time signature for 3 crotchets in a bar is . $\frac{3}{4}$ – *not* $\frac{3}{\rho}$

This is best shown in tabulated form.

No line is used to separate the upper from the lower number, although a time signature observes the principle of an arithmetical vulgar fraction, the top figure (numerator) telling *how many* (beats), and the bottom figure (denominator) telling *what sort* (of beat).

Number of Beats in a Bar	The kind of Note chosen for the Beat (The "One-Beat Note")	The Time Signature	Reason
2	Minim ρ	$\frac{2}{2}$ (or $\frac{2}{\rho}$)	
3	Minim ρ	$\frac{3}{2}$ (or $\frac{3}{\rho}$)	Because there are 2 minims in a semibreve
4	Minim ρ	$\frac{4}{2}$ (or $\frac{4}{\rho}$)	
2	Crotchet	$\frac{2}{4}$ (or $\frac{2}{\rho}$)	
3	Crotchet	$\frac{3}{4}$ (or $\frac{3}{\rho}$)	Because there are 4 crotchets in a semibreve
4	Crotchet	$\frac{4}{4}$ (or $\frac{4}{\rho}$)	
2	Quaver	$\frac{2}{8}$ (or $\frac{2}{\rho}$)	
3	Quaver	$\frac{3}{8}$ (or $\frac{3}{\rho}$)	Because there are 8 quavers in a semibreve
4	Quaver	$\frac{4}{8}$ (or $\frac{4}{\rho}$)	

26. The reason for the other system of naming notes is now plain:—
Semibreve (whole note) = 1 : Minim (half note) = $\frac{1}{2}$
Crotchet (quarter note) = $\frac{1}{4}$: Quaver (eighth note) = $\frac{1}{8}$
Semiquaver (sixteenth note) = $\frac{1}{16}$

27. It is *possible* to have a time of one, two or three semibreves to a bar, in which cases the time signatures would be $\frac{1}{1}$ $\frac{2}{1}$ $\frac{3}{1}$.

16

28. Of the time signatures mentioned so far, $\frac{2}{8}$ is hardly ever used, and $\frac{4}{8}$ infrequently. When a time of 4 quavers to a bar is required, it is generally represented by $\frac{2}{4}$, in which each bar contains the equivalent of 2 crotchets or 4 quavers. Such times as $\frac{2}{16}$ and $\frac{4}{16}$ (2 and 4 semi-quavers) are never used.

29. $\frac{4}{4}$ time (4 crotchets to the bar) is often called **Common Time:** shown thus:—

The above sign is not the letter C from the word " common." It is really a corruption of the sign for a semi-circle. In medieval days triple (or three) time was called " perfect time " because of the analogy with the threefold nature of the Trinity, and was shown by the sign of a perfect circle — O. Duple time was called ' imperfect " and was given a half circle as its sign — C.

The latter sign has been appropriated as the sign meaning $\frac{4}{4}$ time.

30. A line drawn through the " imperfect " sign, thus ₵ is rather ambiguous. It may mean $\frac{2}{2}$, in which case the conductor beats two minim beats to the bar, but it may also mean $\frac{4}{2}$ time.

Simple Time

31. Each beat often divides into two half-beats:—
    A minim beat may divide into two crotchet beats.
    A crotchet beat may divide into two quaver beats.
    A quaver beat may divide into two semiquaver beats.
Such time—*in which each beat divides into two*—is called **simple time.**
(Each beat may sub-divide further into four parts or eight parts, etc.)

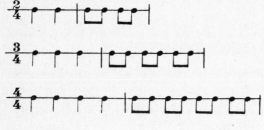

is called
Simple Duple Time
(with crotchet beats)
is called
Simple Triple Time
(with crotchet beats)
is called
Simple Quadruple Time
(with crotchet beats)

32. Similarly:—
    $\frac{2}{2}$ is called Simple Duple Time   (with minim beats)
    $\frac{3}{2}$ is called Simple Triple Time   (with minim beats)
    $\frac{4}{2}$ is called Simple Quadruple Time (with minim beats)
    $\frac{3}{8}$ is called Simple Triple Time   (with quaver beats)
    $\frac{4}{8}$ is called Simple Quadruple Time (with quaver beats)

33. In paragraph 31, the division of beats into half-beats is shown. Beats may further divide into four, eight or even more parts:—

34. Notice how quavers and semiquavers are arranged or grouped according to the beats. The last bar above would be most confusing to the eye if written thus:—

35. While the steady pulse or beat continues unchanged in every bar—that is, while the *time* continues unchanged—the *pattern* of the notes may be always changing as in paragraph 33. The pattern is known as **rhythm** or **rhythmic pattern.** The rhythmic pattern is as it were superimposed on the time.

In marching, all sorts of notes, long and short, may be heard from the band, while the marchers (helped by the bass drum) keep up a steady LEFT - RIGHT - LEFT - RIGHT, being concerned solely with the *time*.

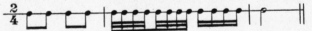

N.B.—*Rhythm* has other meanings such as the swing or verve of music, and the number of bars in a phrase. Such meanings are out of place in a first book on music.

36. Grouping according to the beats is a fairly simple matter so long as no notes shorter than semiquavers are used. There are, however, eight demisemiquavers in a crotchet and eight notes in one group are difficult to read, e.g.:—

In such a case the eight demisemiquavers will be still grouped in one crotchet beat, but they will also be divided into two groups of four each:—

37. Grouping in $\frac{3}{4}$ and $\frac{3}{8}$ time presents no difficulties:—

Here is the same passage in $\frac{3}{8}$ time, the value of all the notes having been halved:—

The first bar of the ⅜ passage could equally well be written:—

but the others are better without a continuous line, for the sake of clearness.

38.   Grouping is not so clear in ²⁄₂, ³⁄₂ and ⁴⁄₂ time because the half-beat notes (crotchets) have no hooks to be joined up:—

N.B.—It is never so easy to read music with *minim* beats as to read music with *crotchet* beats, and that is one reason why *the crotchet is more frequently used than any other note as the " one-beat note."* Once again the drawback of the American system of naming notes will be seen.   The crotchet is so frequently chosen as the " one-beat note " or " whole note " that to call it at the same time the " quarter-note " is confusing.   (See paragraphs 17 and 26.)

39.   Special care is needed in grouping notes in ⁴⁄₄ and ²⁄₂ time, because of the need *to keep clear the division between the two equal parts (two beats each) of each bar.   A fresh group should always mark the beginning of the third beat.*

This would be wrong:—

Half-way mark

The quaver grouping " straddles " or obscures the beginning of the important third beat.

This would be correct:—

Half-way mark

40.   In ²⁄₄ and ³⁄₄ time a whole bar of quavers may be grouped together, their hooks joined in one line.

Thus we can write:—

or

or

In ⅜ time semiquavers can be written:—

or   or

QUESTIONS AND EXERCISES ON CHAPTER III

1. (a) What is meant by " time " in music?
   (b) What is the purpose of the bar-line?
   (c) How is the double bar-line used?

2. (a) How many strong accents occur in a single bar of two-time or three-time?
   (b) What accents occur in a bar of four-time?

3. (a) What is the function or purpose of a time signature?
   (b) Of what does it consist?
   (c) Which figure indicates the number of beats to a bar?
   (d) How is the kind of beat (crotchet, minim, etc.) indicated?

4. Explain these time signatures:—

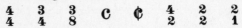

5. What is meant by " simple " time?

6. Write the time signatures corresponding to these descriptions:—

Simple duple time	—	crotchet beats
Simple duple time	—	minim beats
Simple triple time	—	quaver beats
Simple triple time	—	crotchet beats
Simple quadruple time	—	minim beats
Simple quadruple time	—	crotchet beats
Simple quadruple time	—	quaver beats

7. Supply the time signatures for these bars of music:—

8. In the following bars the notes are grouped incorrectly. Re-group them according to the time signatures.

9. Re-write this passage in $\frac{3}{8}$ time, halving the value of all the notes. The number of bars will remain the same:—

10. Re-write this passage in $\frac{4}{2}$ time, doubling the value of all the notes:—

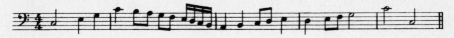

11. What is the difference between time and rhythm?

CHAPTER IV

DOTTED NOTES – RESTS AND
THEIR GROUPING – SYNCOPATION

41. In paragraph 18 a *tie* or *bind* was explained, its effect being to make one long sound equalling the duration of the two notes joined by the curve.

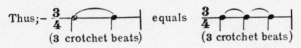

Exactly the same effect (minim plus crotchet) is obtained by putting a **dot** after the minim. A dot placed after any note (that is, to its right) adds half the value of the note:—

A minim	equals	2 crotchets (joined)
A dotted minim	equals	3 crotchets (that is, a minim plus half a minim)
	=	
	=	

42. A dotted crotchet equals 3 quavers (that is a crotchet and a half)

A dotted quaver ·equals 3 semiquavers (a quaver and a half)

A dotted semibreve equals 3 minims (a semibreve and a half)

43. A **second dot** may also be used, this second dot adding half the value of the first dot. Thus, while the first dot adds ½ the value of the note, the second dot adds ¼ the value of the note, and the two dots together add ¾ of the value of the note.

The following examples should make this clear:—

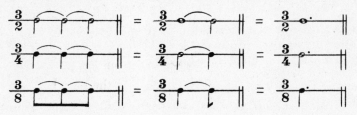

44. The use of dotted notes makes it possible to use a single note to fill a bar of triple time:—

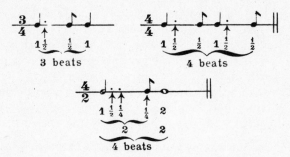

45. Single notes worth $1\frac{1}{2}$ beats or $1\frac{3}{4}$ beats are freely used:—

A combination of dot and tie is often clearer to read than two dots:—

46. In quadruple time where it is always desirable to show clearly the half-way division in the bar, namely, the beginning of the third beat, it is always better to avoid dotting a note across the beginning of the third beat:—

47. Music hardly ever consists of continuous sound: the signs that enjoin the silence of a performer are called **rests.** Every note (minim, crotchet, etc.) has its corresponding rest, so that the duration of a silence is as exactly indicated as the duration of a sound. This is shown in the following table:—

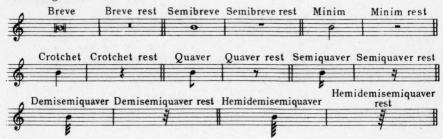

N.B.—(a) Semibreve and minim rests are easily confused. A useful memory-aid is:—

        Semibreve — Suspended (from the line)

        Minim   — Mounted (on the line)

(b) The crotchet rest was formerly like the quaver rest, but with the head turned to the right. The type given above is now universally favoured as being quite distinctive. It resembles an incomplete curly bracket.

(c) The placing of the rests has nothing to do with the pitch-names of the notes. Semibreve, minim and crotchet rests are put as near as possible to the middle of the stave.

The head of the quaver rest generally occupies the third space up.

The number of *heads* in the quaver, semiquaver, demisemiquaver and hemidemisemiquaver rests respectively corresponds to the number of *hooks* in the notes.

48. Although rests *cannot be tied* like notes, *they can be dotted*, the first dot adding half the value, and the second dot adding one-quarter of the value of the rest.

(a) ——— Rest equalling a minim and a half—or three crotchets

(b) ——— Rest equalling a minim and threequarters—or seven quavers

(c) —ξ— Rest equalling a crotchet and a half—or three quavers

(d) —ξ— Rest equalling a crotchet and threequarters—or seven semiquavers

The above periods of silence could equally well have been indicated:—

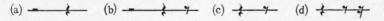

49. **A whole bar's rest** is always shown as a **semibreve rest,** odd though this may seem when used equally for duple, triple and quadruple time, or when the whole bar contains less than the value of a semibreve.

24

A whole bar's rest in $\frac{3}{4}$ time is 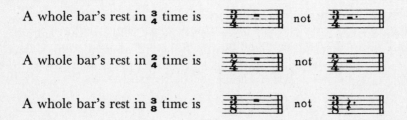 not

A whole bar's rest in $\frac{2}{4}$ time is   not

A whole bar's rest in $\frac{3}{8}$ time is   not

50. **A breve rest** may be met with in church music to indicate a whole bar's rest in $\frac{4}{2}$ time :—

It is a rectangular block filling the space between the third and fourth lines of the stave.

A breve rest is still used in orchestral parts to indicate *two bars' silence.*

A breve rest plus a semibreve rest may represent *three bars'* silence. A **long** (double breve) **rest** may stand for *four bars'* silence. To make everything clear, however, the number of bars' rest is also put over the top :—

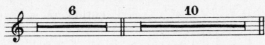

For a longer silence this kind of indication is utilised :—

no attempt being made to write the exact rest value for six or ten bars.

51. There are never any blank spaces in bars of music: the period of silence must be indicated exactly by means of one or more rests.

In this bar $\frac{2}{4}$ the crotchet occupies one beat of the two

required to fill the bar. The remaining one beat space must be filled with a rest :— $\frac{2}{4}$

In this bar $\frac{3}{4}$ only two beats of the three in the bar are

accounted for. The remaining space must be filled with the appropriate rest :— $\frac{3}{4}$

Incomplete bars are, however, found at the beginning of a piece of music when the first note occurs on a beat other than the first, e.g. :—

It is not usual to write :—

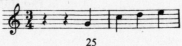

25

In a short passage beginning on a beat other than the first of the bar, it is the custom to leave the last bar incomplete as well as the first, so that the two bars (first and last) make one complete bar:—

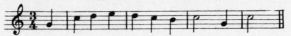

Bar 1 contains one beat.

The last bar contains two beats.

The two together make up three beats according to the time signature.

In a piece of any length, however, the final bar is always complete, no matter what beats are represented in the first bar.

52. All rests added to complete a bar must be grouped according to the time signature, just as with the note grouping shown in paragraphs 34 to 40.

In this example:— $\frac{3}{4}$ the dotted crotchet takes up one and a half beats, leaving one and a half beats to be filled by a rest or rests.

It would be *quite wrong* to complete the bar thus:—

The above will not do because the outline of 3 beats to a bar is completely lost.

The following two rules must be applied:—

(1) Each *beat* must be completed before dealing with the next beat.

(2) Each *part* of a beat must be completed before dealing with next part of a beat.

In the example immediately above, the *first* beat is complete and is left alone, but the second beat is represented by *half* its length (the dot). Applying the second rule, this second beat will be completed by adding a half-beat rest (a quaver rest). The *third* beat is then given a crotchet rest:—

53. In paragraph 39 it was stated that in quadruple time notes should not obscure the beginning of the third beat by being grouped across the half-way mark of the bar. *This rule also applies to rests*, particularly to the *minim rest*:—

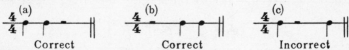

In examples (a) and (b) the beginning of the third beat is unobscured and the two halves of the bar clearly shown.

In example (c) the minim rest straddles the middle of the bar. The correct version would be as follows:—

54. Although the minim *note* is freely used in $\frac{3}{4}$ time

and the crotchet *note* is freely used in $\frac{3}{8}$ time

— the minim *rest* is *not* used in $\frac{3}{4}$ time

and the crotchet *rest* is *not* used in $\frac{3}{8}$ time.

Putting this in general terms—*a two beat rest is not used in three time.*

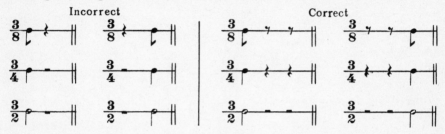

55. When rests have to be inserted *between* given notes the problem becomes more complicated, as in the following examples:—

(a) Complete this bar with rests according to the signature, placing the rests *between* the given notes:

(i) 3 crotchets or 6 quavers to the bar.
(ii) The first quaver must be the first half of the first beat: to complete the first beat, add a quaver rest *after* the note.
(iii) The last quaver must be the second half of the third beat: to Complete this beat, add a quaver rest *before* the note.
This is the result:

(iv) The *first* and *third* beats are complete: it now remains to add a crotchet rest in the middle to represent the missing *second* beat.
This is the final result:

(b) Complete this bar similarly:—

(i) 2 crotchets to the bar.
(ii) The semiquaver is one-quarter of the beat. The first thing to do is therefore to complete half the first beat by adding a semiquaver rest.

27

(iii) Having completed half the first beat, add a quaver rest to complete the other half of the first beat.

1st beat

(iv) Next we *work backwards* from the demisemiquaver, which is one-eighth of the crotchet beat. The first thing to do is to supply a demisemiquaver rest before the demisemiquave-note, thus adding one-eighth of the beat to complete one quarter.

(v) Next add a semiquaver rest (one-quarter of the beat), so as to complete one-half of the beat.

(vi) Finally add a quaver rest to complete with the other half the whole second beat:

2nd beat

The whole bar will now appear thus:—

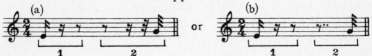

It would be quite legitimate to use dots as in (b), the divisions of the bar, the beats and the parts of the beats being equally clear.

56.   Two more examples are given of rests *following* the given notes:—

(a) Given: $\frac{4}{4}$

(i) The dot after the crotchet is half of the second crotchet beat, therefore add a quaver rest to complete the second beat.

(ii) Beats 1 and 2 are now complete and the half-way mark clearly defined. We simply add a minim rest to complete the bar.

(b) Given: $\frac{4}{2}$

(i) The quaver belongs to the second minim, of which it forms one-quarter.

(ii) First add a quaver rest, in order to complete one-half of the second beat.

(iii) Next add a crotchet rest to complete the remaining half of the second beat.

28

(iv) As the half-way mark of the bar is now clearly defined, the bar is completed by the addition of a semibreve rest:

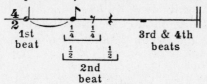

Syncopation

57. The accepted strong beat in duple, triple and quadruple time is the first beat, with a **medium accent** on the third beat of quadruple time.

If the accent is transferred from the first beat (or the third beat in quadruple time) to a normally unaccented beat, the resulting effect is known as **syncopation.**

Syncopation then is **disturbed accent.**

[N.B.—The medical term " syncope " means missing a heart-beat.]

In examples (a) and (b) below there are no notes on the first beats of the bars:—

There is here no real transference of the accent to other beats. In practice the performer would supply the first beat by perhaps nodding the head or stamping the foot to enable him to keep time. This is one type of syncopation.

In the next examples there are *notes sounding* on the strong beat but there are *no notes struck* on the first beats (or third beats in quadruple time)—except in the first bar of (c).

The arrows indicate where the normal accents would fall.

The effect of (c) and (d) in performance would be as follows:—

(The accent sign > is explained in paragraph 19.)

The accents have been transferred to beats which are normally unaccented, the accent being disturbed.

58. It will be observed that syncopation in quadruple time may obscure the beginning of the third beat when the normally unaccented second beat is prolonged across it—as in example (c) in paragraph 57. Paragraph 46, which emphasises the importance of showing clearly the half-way division of the bar in $\frac{4}{4}$ time, does not therefore apply when syncopation is present.

> N.B.—Syncopation has been in common use for centuries, so that the claim sometimes made by purveyors of what has been variously known as 20th century " rag-time," " jazz " or " swing " to have " invented " it has no validity.

59. Syncopation can also occur *inside* the beat.
In a four-semiquaver group the first and third semiquavers would normally take what accent there was.

> In (a) below the second semiquaver of each group usurps the usual accent given to the third semiquaver.
> In (b) below there is no first semiquaver in each group, the third semiquaver is also blanketed, and the syncopation even more marked than in (a).

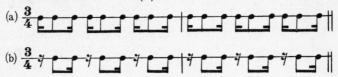

QUESTIONS AND EXERCISES ON CHAPTER IV

1. (a) What is the effect of placing a dot after a note?
   (b) What is the effect of placing two dots after a note?

2. By making use of dots write the following:—
   (a) One note equal in length to three minims.
   (b) One note equal in length to three crotchets.
   (c) One note equal in length to three quavers.
   (d) One note equal in length to six quavers.
   (e) One note equal in length to seven quavers.
   (f) One note equal in length to seven semiquavers.
   (g) One note equal in length to twelve demisemiquavers.
   (h) One note equal in length to fourteen semiquavers.

3. Re-write these bars, using ties instead of dots:—

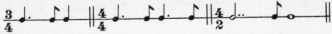

4. What are rests?

5. Write on the treble stave the rests corresponding to these notes:—
   minim, demisemiquaver, crotchet, semibreve, semiquaver, quaver.

6. Name these rests:—

7. On the bass stave write the following:—
   (a) A rest worth four quavers.
   (b) A rest worth six quavers.
   (c) A rest worth seven quavers.
   (d) A rest worth four demisemiquavers.
   (e) A rest worth six demisemiquavers.
   (f) A rest worth seven demisemiquavers.

8. What do the following mean?

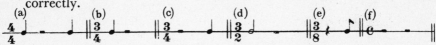

9. (a) What rest is generally used for a whole bar's silence?
   (b) What rest could be used in $\frac{4}{2}$ time for a whole bar's silence?

10. What is wrong with the following? Then re-write the examples correctly.

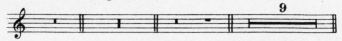

11. Complete these bars with rests. In section (a) the rests are to be added *after* the notes; in section (b) *before* the notes; and in section (c) *between* the two sets of notes.

12. Add the respective time signatures to these bars, and describe the kind of time in each case (simple duple, etc.):—

13. (a) What is syncopation?
   (b) Write a bar containing syncopation in $\frac{4}{4}$ time.
   (c) Write a bar containing syncopation in $\frac{3}{4}$ time.
       [Write the rhythm only, using one line for the notes: no melody is required.]

31

14. According to the given time signature add bar-lines to these passages, each of which consists of a number of complete bars. Each passage begins on the first beat of the bar.

(a)

(b)

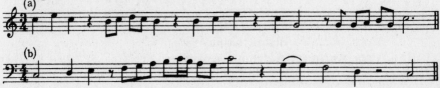

15. Re-write this passage:—
    (a) In $\frac{3}{8}$ time, halving the value of each note and rest.
    (b) In $\frac{3}{2}$ time, doubling the value of each note and rest.
    In each case there will be no change in the number of bars.

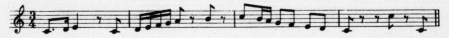

CHAPTER V

THE MAJOR SCALE — SHARPS AND FLATS — TONALITY OR SENSE OF KEY — TECHNICAL NAMES OF THE DEGREES OF THE SCALE

60. Everyone will be familiar with the series of what are called "sol-fa" notes, viz., doh, ray, me, fah, soh, lah, te, doh. This has been described as a *ladder of sounds*. The Italian word for " ladder " is " scala," and this ladder of sounds is called a **scale.**

The " sol-fa syllables," as they are called, consist of seven differently named notes, which can be repeated at various pitches. In paragraph 2 the piano keyboard is described as consisting of a series of seven notes constantly repeating themselves higher up or lower down, and each eighth note is said to be an " octave " above or below the next note of the same name. Paragraph 2 deals only with the white notes of the keyboard, which were given alphabetical names.

61. If we know on which note to begin and end, it is possible to play on the white notes of the piano keyboard a scale which sounds just like *doh ray* . . . up to " top doh. An experienced pianist, by using white *and* black notes, is able to begin on *any* note of the piano and play a scale sounding like the sol-fa scale, but there is only *one note* we can choose as " doh " (the first and last note of the scale) to produce the required effect *on white notes only*. Every other attempt will need one or more black notes to make the series sound correct. That one note is **C.**

The series C D E F G A B C—all white notes—sounds exactly like *d r m f s l t d'*.

62. This series on the white notes from C to the next C is called the **major scale.**

> N.B.—" Major " means " bigger ": the opposite word "minor", which will be met with later, means " lesser ". The *Major* Scale is so called because the distance C to E (or *doh* to *me*) on white notes forms the " interval " of a *Major* Third. *Intervals* are explained in Chapters VIII and IX.

63. Because this scale begins and ends on C (C being its *doh* or **tonic**) it is called the **scale of C major**, and music which makes use of the Scale of C major is said to be in the **Key of C major.**

> N.B.—In paragraph 4 the word *Key* is also used to describe the wooden levers (white and black) which make up the pianoforte keyboard.

64. When we begin to learn to play the piano, we try music in Key C first, because it is the easiest to understand, consisting as it does entirely of white notes. Next we make the acquaintance of the scale which contains one black note, then one with two black notes, and so on, until we can read music in any scale or key.

This diagram shows the notes forming the scale of C with the corresponding musical notation below it:—

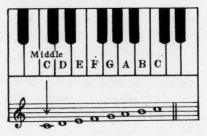

65. Notice that between E and F, and between B and C *there is no black note*. This is because E and F, and B and C, are so close together in *pitch* that there is no room for a keyboard note between them. Although it does not appear to be so on the keyboard diagram above, E is as close to F in pitch as F is close to the black note immediately to its right.

The distance or difference in pitch from middle C to the black note immediately to its right is called a **semitone** or half-tone, and the pitch distance from that black note to the next white note, D, is also called a *semitone* or half-tone. The pitch distance from white note C to white note D is therefore called a **whole tone** or simply a **tone**.

66. The distance E to F and the distance B to C are semitones just like the distance—middle C to the black note to its right. These distances or differences in pitch are called **intervals**, which are explained fully in Chapters VIII and IX.

The construction of the major scale is therefore:—

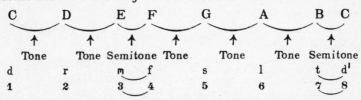

67. It is usual to mark semitones with little curves as shown above, but not to mark tones with large curves.

In a major scale semitones occur between notes 3 and 4, and notes 7 and 8—whatever note is chosen as the *doh* or *tonic* or starting and finishing note.

The major scale really consists of two groups of *four* notes each, each group being in alphabetical order, and each being called a **tetrachord** (" tetra " is a Greek word meaning four). Each tetrachord consists of tone—tone—semitone, and the *lower tetrachord* is separated from the *upper tetrachord* by a tone:—

Lower Tetrachord   Upper Tetrachord

68. Although the scale of C major consists entirely of white notes, melodies in that key *often bring in black notes* as a kind of decoration or ornament to the tune. The most common black note to be introduced in this way is the black note to the right of F, that is, the note a semitone higher than F. This black note takes its name from F and may be described as *F raised*. In music this raising a note by a semitone is called *sharpening*. This black note then is *F sharpened*, or simply **F sharp**. *The sign for a sharp is* ♯. It is always *placed before*, never after, the note. We *say* " F sharp ", but we *write* " sharp F ", thus:—

69. When it is desired to bring back the white note F, a sign called a **natural**— ♮ — is used, thus:—

black   white

70. Although a black note may be used in a piece of music in Key C— not as a note of the key but as a kind of decoration or ornament—it must be immediately followed by the corresponding white note, otherwise the music will no longer be in Key C. If we continue using F sharp without contradiction, the effect will be that of changing to another key.

71. Leaving key C we next tackle a key or scale containing one black note. There are *two* such scales or keys. To find the first we take the *upper tetrachord* of the scale of C (see paragraph 67) and make it the *lower tetrachord* of a new scale—adding a new tetrachord above it:—

Formerly Upper Tetrachord   New Upper Tetrachord
of C   finishing on G
- now Lower Tetrachord
of a scale starting
on G

72. As this scale begins and ends on G, it will be called the scale of G. If we play it, however, we shall find that the last note but one (F) " sounds wrong." If we sing the scale " *d r m f s l t d¹* " while we play, there will be a clash when we sing " te." The reason is that the pattern of tones and semitone is not correct in the upper tetrachord. It *should* be:— tone—tone—semitone, but with white notes only the pattern is as follows:—

D   E   F   G

5   6   7   8

The semitone comes between 6 and 7 instead of between 7 and 8. To obtain the correct pattern we must substitute *F sharp* for F, thus making the required tone between E and F sharp, and the required semitone between F sharp and G:—

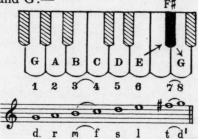

This Scale of G (or Key of G—G being called the **key-note**) has the note F sharp as a *permanent* member, instead of the white note F.

73. To establish the other scale which needs one black note we take the *lower tetrachord* of the scale of C (see paragraph 67), and make it the *upper tetrachord* of a new scale, adding a new tetrachord below it:—

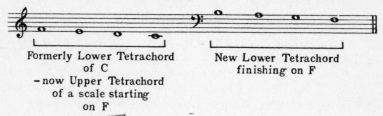

Formerly Lower Tetrachord
of C
– now Upper Tetrachord
of a scale starting
on F

New Lower Tetrachord
finishing on F

For convenience we write the scale ascending in the treble clef throughout and an octave higher:—

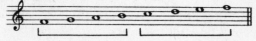

As it begins and ends on F, it will be called the scale of F, F being its *key-note*. But if we play it as it stands, we shall find that the fourth note up (B) "sounds wrong." If we sing the scale "*d r m f s l t d¹*" while we play, there will be a clash on the note "fah." The reason once again is that the pattern of tones and semitone is not correct in the lower tetrachord. It *should* be:—tone—tone—semitone, but with white notes only the pattern is as follows:—

This pattern consists entirely of *tones*.

The fourth note B is *too high in pitch*, and to obtain the correct pattern we substitute the black note to the left of B for the white note B. This black note takes its name from B and may be described as *B lowered*. In music lowering a note by a semitone is called *flattening*. This black note then is *B flattened* or simply **B flat**. Like the *sharp* or *natural* the flat— ♭ —is always *placed before* the note. We *say* "B flat," but we *write* "flat B."

The following keyboard diagram shows the process followed in arriving at the formation of the Scale of F:—

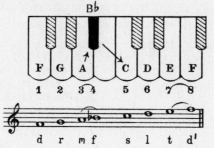

74. { Because in the scale of G, F sharp, and not F, is a regular member of the scale—
Because in the scale of F, B flat, and not B, is a regular member of the scale—

    then

The sharp in Key G ⎫ are written *once* at the beginning so as to
    and   ⎬ avoid the constant writing of sharp or
The flat in Key F ⎭ flat before F or B respectively.

F sharp   -   B flat

N.B.—It is very important to place the sharp, flat or natural on the line or in the space of the note whose name it takes. The following would be incorrect:

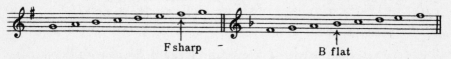

Scale of G   Scale of F

In (*a*) the sharp is in the E space and stands for E sharp—not F sharp as required.

In (*b*) the flat is on the D line and stands for D flat—not B flat as required.

The lateral (crosswise) lines of the sharp or natural should be one on each side of the note line, or they should exactly enclose the space.

♯ or ♯

♭ or ♭

♮ or ♮

75. Sharps or flats placed at the beginning of a piece of music to indicate the key make what is called the **key signature.**

76. The *key signature* appears at *the beginning of every line of music.*
The *time signature* (see paragraph 24) appears *in the first bar only*
unless the time changes in the course of the piece.
The key signature always precedes the time signature:—

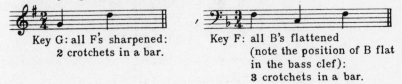

Key G: all F's sharpened: Key F: all B's flattened
2 crotchets in a bar.   (note the position of B flat
in the bass clef):
3 crotchets in a bar.

N.B.—The *absence* of any sharps or flats is the " key signature "
of key C.

77. Sharps, flat or naturals frequently appear in a piece of music
though not present in the key signature—for example, F sharp in key C, B flat
in key C, B natural in key F.
Such sharps, flats or naturals are called **accidentals.** Accidentals
*affect all the notes of the same alphabetical name at the same pitch that follow them
in the same bar,* unless contradicted:—

F *natural* –   B *flat* –
though not marked   though not marked

Note that, in key G above, the F sharp *signature* on the top line
applies equally to the F note in the bottom space. However,
the *accidental* F natural in the bottom space would not have
affected an F note on the top line. Key *signatures* affect all
notes *at all pitches. Accidentals* affect notes *at the same pitch* only.

78. Because major scales consist largely of tones, or, as we say, because
they *proceed* mainly *through* tones, they are called **diatonic** (Greek *dia*,
meaning " through ": Greek *tonos*, meaning " tone "). In Chapter VII
" minor " scales are dealt with: these are also *diatonic. Diatonic music* is
music written in major and minor keys (which proceed or move mainly
" through tones ").
The opposite word to diatonic is **chromatic** (see Chapter IX).

79. To find the key with two sharps we take the *upper* tetrachord of
the scale of G and make it the *lower* tetrachord of the new scale starting
on D, which note gives its name to the scale or key:—

Lower Tetrachord of   Upper Tetrachord of
G   G

For convenience we drop down an octave, and again we need to sharpen
the seventh note (c) to obtain the right pattern of tones and semitones.
The F sharp is taken over from Key G:—

(a) above is incorrect, the semitone occurring between 6 and 7 instead of 7 and 8

(b) is correct, the semitone occurring between 7 and 8, but the new note, C sharp, is written as an *accidental*

(c) shows the new key signature of two sharps (F sharp and C sharp) for the key of D.

N.B.—Each new sharp is placed to the right of the one before.

80. To find the key with two flats we take the *lower* tetrachord of the scale of F and make it the *upper* tetrachord of the new scale:—

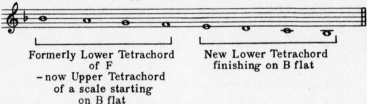

Formerly Lower Tetrachord
of F
– now Upper Tetrachord
of a scale starting
on B flat

New Lower Tetrachord
finishing on B flat

This new scale begins and ends on a black note and will be called the scale of B flat.

As in paragraph 73 we now write the scale ascending with the notes in alphabetical order:—

(a) is incorrect, because of the semitone between 4 and 5, instead of 3 and 4.

(b) is correct, the fourth note (E) having been flattened to ensure that the semitone comes between 3 and 4: the new note, E flat, is written as an *accidental*.

(c) shows the new key signature of two flats (B flat and E flat) for the key of B flat.

N.B.—Each new flat is placed to the right of the one before. The E flat in the key signature *could* have been put on the bottom line, but the custom is to put it in the top space.

81. The order of sharp keys from key C is seen to be:—C, G, D, and it should be observed that G is the *fifth* note above C, and D is the *fifth* note above G. Each succeeding key-note of a scale possessing one more sharp than its predecessor will be found to be the *fifth* note above the previous key-note. Each new sharp also will be found to be *five* places above the last sharp previously added.

The following diagram illustrates the use of the number **5** in finding the key-notes of successive sharp keys;—

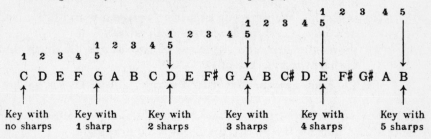

N.B. The seventh note of each new scale is sharpened

82. The order of flat keys from key C is seen to be:—C, F, B (flat), and it should be remembered that we approached flat keys *downwards*, by adding a *lower* tetrachord. The *fifth* note principle therefore applies to flat keys, F being the *fifth* note below C and Bb the *fifth* note below F. Reckoning downwards involves counting backwards, which is confusing (e.g. C B A G *F*). By counting four *upwards* we shall arrive at the same note as by counting five *downwards* (e.g. C D E *F*). Each succeeding key-note of a scale possessing one more flat than its predecessor will be found to be the *fourth* note above the previous key-note. Each new flat also will be found to be *four* places above the last flat previously added. It must also be remembered that in proceeding from one flat key to the next, the *fourth* note of the old key has always to be flattened to become the key-note of the new key: in other words, every key-note after F will be a black note—a flat.

The following diagram illustrates the use of the number **4** in finding the key-notes of successive flat keys;—

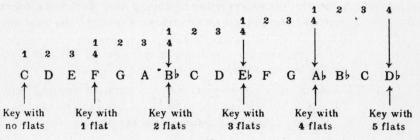

83. Below are all the sharp keys or scales written without key signatures, but indicating the sharps as accidentals: each new sharp (always the last but one note) is marked by an asterisk:—

G major (one sharp)   D major (two sharps)   A major (three sharps)

E major (four sharps)   B major (five sharps)   F♯ major (six sharps)

C♯ major (seven sharps)

Notes on the above scales:

(i) Once a sharp has been used, it appears in all subsequent sharp keys.

(ii) As there are only seven different notes in the major scale, there cannot be a scale with *more* than seven sharps.

(iii) In F sharp major the note E sharp is a *white* note. In C sharp major the notes E sharp and B sharp are *white* notes. This use of white notes as sharps is explained in Chapter VII.

(iv) When a sharp key does not appear to be a fifth note higher than its predecessor, this is in order to keep the scale conveniently on the stave. For instance, the scale of D above begins *four notes below* the scale of G, but counting 4 down or 5 above results in the same alphabetical note.

84. Below are given the key signatures corresponding to the scales in paragraph 83. If these had been used there would have been no accidentals present. Each new sharp is placed to the right of its predecessors, but whether it appears as fifth higher or a fourth lower (which means the same thing) depends upon custom or the limitations of the stave:—

G   D   A   E   B   F♯   C♯

85. We now write all the flat keys without key signatures, but indicating the flats as accidentals: each new flat (always the fourth note up) is marked by an asterisk. This time the bass clef is used:—

F major (one flat)　　Bb major (two flats)　　Eb major (three flats)

Ab major (four flats)　　Db major (five flats)　　Gb major (six flats)

Cb major (seven flats)

Notes on the above scales:

(i) Once a flat has been used it appears in all subsequent flat keys.

(ii) As there are only seven different notes in the major scale, there cannot be a scale with more than seven flats.

(iii) In G flat major the note C flat is a *white* note. In C flat major the notes C flat and F flat are *white* notes. This use of white notes as flats is explained in Chapter VII.

(iv) When a flat key does not appear to be a fourth note higher than its predecessor, this is in order to keep the scale conveniently on the stave. For instance the scale of A flat begins five notes below the scale of E flat, but counting 5 down or 4 up results in the same alphabetical note.

(v) The scales of B major (5 sharps) and C flat major (7 flats) are exactly the same on the piano keyboard.
The scales of F sharp major (6 sharps) and G flat major (6 flats) are exactly the same on the piano keyboard.
The scales of C sharp major (7 sharps) and D flat major (5 flats) are exactly the same on the piano keyboard.
Chapter VII provides the explanation.

86. We now write the key signatures corresponding to the scales in paragraph 85. If these had been used, there would have been no accidentals present. Each new flat is placed to the right of its predecessors, but whether it appears a fourth higher or a fifth lower (which means the same thing) depends upon custom or the limitations of the stave.

F　Bb　Eb　Ab　Db　Gb　Cb

87. The key signature acts as a pointer to the key note. Since the last sharp in a sharp signature is always the *seventh* degree (last but one)

42

of the scale, the key note can always be located by going *one note* (*a semitone*) *higher:*—

G   D   A   E   B

88. In the case of a flat key signature, since the last flat is always the *fourth* degree of the scale, the key note can be located by counting down 4 from it:—

But there is a much easier way: in every key with more than one flat the *last flat but one is itself the key-note.*

B♭   E♭   A♭   D♭

89. The seven degrees of the diatonic scale bear certain *technical names*. The **key-note or " doh "** is called the **tonic** (There is also the term **tonality** which means " sense or feeling of key." There would be no tonality or consciousness of any definite key in a confused mass of sharps and flats thrown together at all sorts of pitches).

The fifth degree (always counting upward) is called the **dominant** (corresponding to " soh " in the solfa notation). It is true to say that this is a *dominating* note of great importance in the scale:—

Dominant ⎤
Tonic   ⎦ in Key C

90. Since the fifth degree *up* is called the *dominant*, the fifth degree *down* is logically called the under-dominant or **subdominant**. In the key of C the subdominant is the note F. Instead of showing it as a fifth below middle C, we show it as the fourth degree of the ascending scale:—

Dominant   Subdominant
Tonic   -   -
Subdominant

91. The mid-way note E is called the **mediant** (the word means " middle " or " go-between.")

As the third degree *upward* is called the *mediant*, the third degree *down* will be called the **submediant**.

Dominant   Showing A, the submediant
Mediant   in its place as the sixth degree
Tonic   -   of the ascending scale.
Submediant

N.B.—This explanation should help students who may be puzzled because the sub (or under) mediant appears in the scale *above the mediant* itself.

92.   Five notes of the seven have now been accounted for: there remain the second and seventh degrees.

The second, being immediately *above the tonic* is called the **supertonic** ("super" meaning *above*).

The seventh, which always gives a strong impression of wanting *to lead to the tonic*, is called the **leading note.**

All the technical names are given below:—

1	2	3	4	5	6	7	8
Tonic	Supertonic	Mediant	Subdominant	Dominant	Submediant	leading Note	Tonic

93.   Examination questions on scales sometimes require the scales to begin *on a note other than the tonic*. In such cases it is well to mark the semitones for guidance, thus:—

Question: *Write on the bass stave the scale of B major, beginning on the submediant.*   Use the key signature.

Method of   The notes of this scale of five sharps are:—
Working:

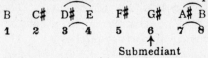

B   C♯   D♯ E   F♯   G♯   A♯ B
1   2   3 4   5   6   7 8
                    ↑
                 Submediant

Answer:

6   7   8
        or
1   2   3   4   5   6

94.   The following type of question is not usually given in examination papers, though it provides a useful exercise:—

Question: *These large and small curves represent the scale of A flat major, but the scale does not begin and end on the tonic.   At each point (where curve meets curve) write the correct names of the notes:—*

Method of   A flat major runs as follows:—
Working:

1   2   3   4   5   6   7   8

A♭   B♭   C   D♭   E♭   F   G   A♭

As the question starts with three full curves (representing *three full tones*), the first note cannot be the tonic. Referring to the major scale pattern we notice that three full tones begin on the fourth degree.

Answer: The answer therefore is:—

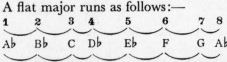

4   5   6   7   8   2   3   4

D♭   E♭   F   G   A♭   B♭   C   D♭
                    ↑
                 Tonic

The semitones are seen to occur the correct places, between 3 and 4 and 7 and 8.

44

QUESTIONS AND EXERCISES ON CHAPTER V.

1. What is meant by a scale?

2. (a) What note must be chosen as the starting and finishing note if the scale is to sound like the solfa scale *d ... d'*, using white notes only?
   (b) What is this scale called?
   (c) Describe the construction of the major scale in its order of tones and semitones.

3. (a) What is meant by a tetrachord?
   (b) What is the arrangement of tones and semitones in a tetrachord?
   (c) Write the scale of C major (one octave beginning on middle C) marking the tetrachords.

4. (a) What is meant by sharpening a note?
   (b) What is meant by flattening a note?
   (c) What contradicts a sharp or a flat?

5. Is it possible to use black notes in key C, and, if so, in what way?

6. What two major scales each contain one black note only?

7. How is key G built up from key C?

8. How is key F built up from key C?

9. (a) What degree of a key or scale must always be sharpened to produce the scale with one sharp more?
   (b) What degree of a key or scale must always be flattened to produce the scale with one flat more?

10. (a) What is a key signature?
    (b) Where is it placed and how often is it written?
    (c) Which is placed first, the key signature or the time signature?

11. (a) What is an accidental?
    (b) Which notes does it affect and for how long?

12. What is meant by a diatonic scale?

13. (a) Give the order of the " sharp " keys, beginning with key G as the key with one sharp.
    (b) Which note constantly becomes the key-note of the key with one sharp more?

14. (a) Give the order of the " flat " keys, beginning with F as the key with one flat.
    (b) Which note (after being changed in a certain way) constantly becomes the key-note of the key with one flat more?
    (c) What has to be done each time to this note before it can become the satisfactory key-note of the new scale?

15. Write these scales on the treble and bass staves bracketed together: do not use key signatures but place the sharps and flats before the notes needing them. Mark the semitones with a slur.

> A major, B major, E major;
> A flat major, D flat major, E flat major.

16. Which sharp keys respectively use the same notes on the piano keyboard as:—

> C flat major, G flat major, D flat major?

17. Complete the following major scales by adding the necessary sharps or flats as accidentals:—

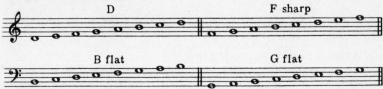

18. Write the key signatures of these major scales, using treble and bass staves bracketed together:—

> A, E, B flat, A flat, G flat, D, F sharp.

In each case write the key-note or tonic as a semibreve.

19. These key signatures all have something wrong about their arrangement. Re-arrange them correctly and state for what keys they stand:—

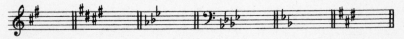

20. How do key signatures act as pointers to the key-notes? Give one or two examples, from flat keys as well as sharp keys.

21. What is meant by " tonality "?

22. Give the technical names of the degrees of the scale.

23. Write in minims with key signatures on the treble stave, one octave ascending, these major scales, and mark the semitones with a slur:—

> D, E, F sharp, B flat, A flat, D flat.

Be careful of the direction of the stems (see paragraph 14).

24. Write in quavers (with separate hooks) with key signatures on the bass stave, one octave descending, these major scales. Mark the semitones with a slur, and be careful of the direction of the stems:—

> A, B, C sharp, E flat, G flat.

25. Write in semibreves with key signatures on the treble stave, one octave ascending:—

> F major beginning and ending on the leading note;
> E flat major beginning and ending on the submediant;
> D major beginning and ending on the dominant;
> E major beginning and ending on the supertonic.

26. Write in semibreves with key signatures on the bass stave, one octave descending:—

B flat major beginning and ending on the subdominant;
A flat major beginning and ending on the mediant;
A major beginning and ending on the leading note;
B major beginning and ending on the dominant.

27. The following diagram (large curves representing tones and small curves representing semitones) shows the pattern of F major beginning on a note other than the tonic. Supply the correct alphabetical names of the notes at the points where curves join, and then state the technical name of the degree of the scale on which the series of notes begins and finishes:—

28. Write the following scales on both staves bracketed, one octave ascending and descending. Group the notes according to the given time signatures, insert bar-lines, and, if the second bar in any example is incomplete, add rests in proper order to complete the bar:—

(a) $\frac{4}{4}$ time—G major in quavers (joined in twos)

$\frac{3}{4}$ time—D major in semiquavers (joined in fours)

$\frac{2}{4}$ time—D flat major in semiquavers (joined in fours)

CHAPTER VI

IRREGULAR NOTE-GROUPS – COMPOUND TIME

95. In paragraph 31 **simple time** was defined as time in which each beat *divides into two parts* (and further subdivides by two). It is possible, however, in simple time for a beat to divide into *three parts*, but such a group of three notes is irregular.

An *irregular group of three notes* used in a simple time is called a **triplet**. A triplet must be played in the time of the " regular " two of the same kind of notes. The three notes forming the triplet must be grouped together and the number " 3 " placed above or below them to show that they form an irregular group, thus:—

Irregular Grouping

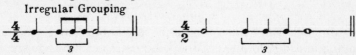

96. Very frequently it is desired to *divide the beat into three parts throughout a piece of music*. The three-note group then ceases to be irregular and becomes regular.

If each beat divides into *three semiquavers*, the whole beat must equal a *dotted quaver*: if each beat divides into *three quavers*, the whole beat must equal a *dotted crotchet*: if each beat divides into *three crotchets*, the whole beat must equal a *dotted minim*.

Time which consistently uses *dotted notes* as beats, each dividing into *three*, is called **compound time**, as distinct from simple time, which consistently uses *undotted notes* as beats, each dividing into *two*.

97. On the left hand side below are examples of *simple duple, simple triple* and *simple quadruple time* with *crotchet* beats; on the right hand side are examples of the corresponding *compound* times with *dotted crotchet* beats. These compound times will be called **compound duple, compound triple** and **compound quadruple** times.

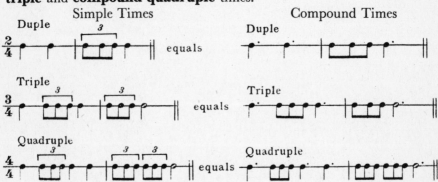

98. The **time signatures of compound times** are more difficult to understand than those of simple times (see paragraph 25). It is impossible to express a dotted crotchet—or indeed any dotted note—

48

as a part of a semibreve using whole numbers only. There are 4 crotchets in a semibreve, but $2\frac{2}{3}$ dotted crotchets in that standard measure of time.

Whereas the time signature for 2 crotchets in a bar is $\frac{2}{4}$, the time signature for 2 *dotted crotchets* would be $\frac{2}{2\frac{2}{3}}$ which would look very odd.

The time signature of a compound time therefore *ignores the main beats* and refers instead to the notes which make up the groups of three.

The compound time:—

is considered as a bar of quavers:—

instead of a bar of two dotted crotchets.

Since there are 8 quavers to a semibreve, the time signature for 6 quavers to a bar is $\frac{6}{8}$.

Similarly:—

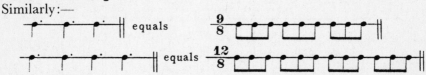

99. Every simple time has its corresponding compound time, whatever the main dotted beat may be—quaver, crotchet or minim. Referring back to paragraph 24, the most sensible way of showing compound time signatures would be:—

With the quaver as the main dotted beat

$\frac{2}{}$, $\frac{3}{}$, $\frac{4}{}$ — but we use $\frac{6}{16}$, $\frac{9}{16}$, $\frac{12}{16}$

With the crotchet as the main dotted beat

$\frac{2}{}$, $\frac{3}{}$, $\frac{4}{}$ — but we use $\frac{6}{8}$, $\frac{9}{8}$, $\frac{12}{8}$

With the minim as the main dotted beat

$\frac{2}{}$, $\frac{3}{}$, $\frac{4}{}$ — but we use $\frac{6}{4}$, $\frac{9}{4}$, $\frac{12}{4}$

100. The following table shows simple and compound times side by side:—

(i) With Quaver or Dotted Quaver as the Main Beat

Kind of Time	Number of Main Beats in a Bar	SIMPLE			COMPOUND		
		Time Signature	Value of Main Beat	Specimen Bars	Time Signature	Value of Main Beat	Specimen Bars
Duple	2	$\frac{2}{8}$	♪		$\frac{6}{16}$	♪.	
Triple	3	$\frac{3}{8}$	♪		$\frac{9}{16}$	♪.	
Quadruple	4	$\frac{4}{8}$	♪		$\frac{12}{16}$	♪.	

49

(ii) With Crotchet or Dotted Crotchet as the Main Beat

← SIMPLE → ← COMPOUND →

Kind of Time	Number of Main Beats in a Bar	Time Signature	Value of Main Beat	Specimen Bars	Time Signature	Value of Main Beat	Specimen Bars
Duple	2	2/4	♩	♩ ♩ ♫ ♫	6/8	♩.	♩. ♩. ♬♬ ♬♬
Triple	3	3/4	♩	♩ ♩ ♩ ♫ ♫ ♫	9/8	♩.	♩. ♩. ♩. ♬♬ ♬♬ ♬♬
Quadruple	4	4/4	♩	♩ ♩ ♩ ♩ ♫ ♫ ♫ ♫	12/8	♩.	♩. ♩. ♩. ♩. ♬♬ ♬♬ ♬♬ ♬♬

(iii) With Minim or Dotted Minim as the Main Beat

← SIMPLE → ← COMPOUND →

Kind of Time	Number of Main Beats in a Bar	Time Signature	Value of Main Beat	Specimen Bars	Time Signature	Value of Main Beat	Specimen Bars
Duple	2	2/2	𝅗𝅥	𝅗𝅥 𝅗𝅥 ♩ ♩ ♩ ♩	6/4	𝅗𝅥.	𝅗𝅥. 𝅗𝅥. ♩ ♩ ♩ ♩ ♩ ♩
Triple	3	3/2	𝅗𝅥	𝅗𝅥 𝅗𝅥 𝅗𝅥 ♩♩♩♩♩♩	9/4	𝅗𝅥.	𝅗𝅥. 𝅗𝅥. 𝅗𝅥. ♩♩♩♩♩♩♩♩♩
Quadruple	4	4/2	𝅗𝅥	𝅗𝅥 𝅗𝅥 𝅗𝅥 𝅗𝅥 ♩♩♩♩♩♩♩♩	12/4	𝅗𝅥.	𝅗𝅥. 𝅗𝅥. 𝅗𝅥. 𝅗𝅥. ♩♩♩♩♩♩♩♩♩♩♩♩

101. In paragraph 54 it was stated that, although a two-beat *note* is freely used in triple time (semibreve in 3/2, minim in 3/4, crotchet in 3/8), yet the corresponding two beat *rest* is *not* used in triple time. As compound time involves the division of the main beats into three parts, much care is needed in the use and grouping of rests. In 6/8 time the crotchet rest is used only when the *first two* (quaver) pulses of the main dotted crotchet beat are silent:—

If the *second and third* (quaver) pulses are silent they must be indicated as *two separate quaver rests:*—

A main beat rest may be written as a dotted crotchet rest, or a crotchet rest plus a quaver rest may be substituted:—

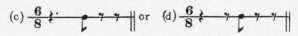

102. The examples in paragraph 101 would appear thus in $\frac{6}{16}$ time:—

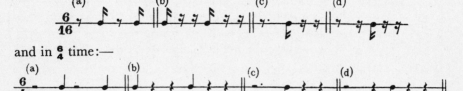

and in $\frac{6}{4}$ time:—

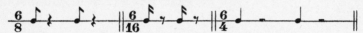

103. The following would be incorrect:—

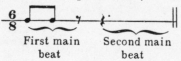

The same rules apply to $\frac{9}{8}$, $\frac{12}{8}$, $\frac{9}{16}$, $\frac{12}{16}$ and $\frac{9}{4}$ times.

($\frac{12}{16}$ time is very rare and $\frac{12}{4}$ practically never used)

104. The rule (given in paragraphs 39 and 53), that in simple quadruple time the half-way division (beginning of the third beat) must not be obscured, applies with equal force to compound quadruple time.

Examples (a), (c) and (d) below are correct, while (b) and (e) are incorrect:—

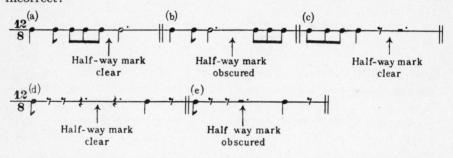

105. Exercises in completing bars with rests are a little more complicated in compound time than in simple time but the same principle applies:—

    (1) complete each beat before passing on to the next;
    (2) complete each part of a beat before passing on to the next part.

Example: Complete this bar with rests:—

Working: In $\frac{6}{8}$ time there are two groups of 3 quavers each.
    Complete the first group with a quaver rest, then complete the bar with a dotted crotchet rest, which will show the division of the bar quite clearly:—

Example: Complete this bar with rests:—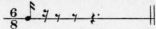

Working: (i) Complete the first quaver beat with a semiquaver rest;

        (ii) complete the first group of 3 quavers (first main dotted crotchet beat) with two quavers rest;

        (iii) complete the bar with a dotted crotchet rest:—

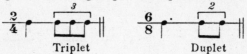

Example: Complete this bar with rests:—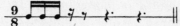

Working: (i) Complete the second quaver beat with a semiquaver rest;

        (ii) complete the first group of 3 quavers with a quaver rest;

        (iii) complete the bar with two dotted crotchet rests.

(A dotted minim rest is not used in $\frac{9}{8}$ time, just as a minim rest is not used in $\frac{3}{4}$ time.)

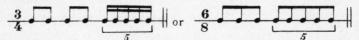

106. Just as an irregular *three-note* group in a *simple time* is called a triplet, so an irregular *two-note* group in a *compound time* is called a **duplet**.

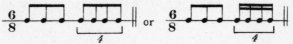

107. Other irregular note-groups are:—

Quadruplet—four notes in the time of three or six of the same kind:—

or

Quintuplet—five notes in the time of three or four of the same kind:—

or

There are others with more notes in the irregular groups. *In every case the irregularity is indicated by the figure placed over or under the group.*

Irregular groups of six notes are called **sextuplets or sextolets**.

Those containing seven notes are called **septuplets or septolets**.

108. In addition to the time signatures already met with there are the less used time signatures such as $\frac{5}{4}$, $\frac{7}{4}$ and $\frac{7}{8}$:

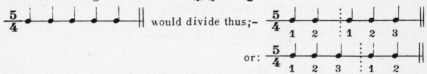

would divide thus:—

or:

52

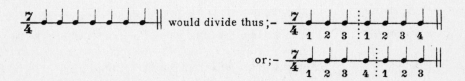 would divide thus;–

QUESTIONS AND EXERCISES ON CHAPTER VI.

1. (a) What is a triplet?
   (b) Write an example (i) in quavers, (ii) in semiquavers.

2. (a) Explain the difference between compound time and simple time.
   (b) Write a bar (i) in compound duple time, (ii) in compound triple time, (iii) in compound quadruple time, using the dotted crotchet as the main beat in each case.

3. Why is it necessary to use a different method to indicate compound time signatures from that used in simple times?

4. Write the following signatures:—
   (a) Compound duple with the dotted minim as the main beat;
   (b) Compound triple with the dotted minim as the main beat;
   (c) Compound duple with the dotted quaver as the main beat;
   (d) Compound triple with the dotted quaver as the main beat.

5. Complete these bars by adding rests *after* the given notes:—

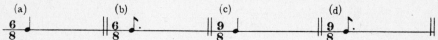

Complete these bars by adding rests *between* the given notes:—

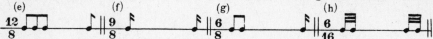

Complete these bars by adding rests *before* the given notes:—

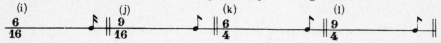

6. Supply time signatures to the following:—

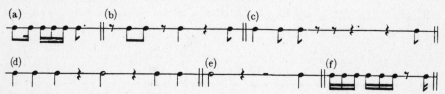

7. What compound time signatures correspond to these simple time signatures:—

$$\frac{2}{4} \quad \frac{3}{4} \quad \frac{2}{2} \quad \frac{3}{8} \quad \frac{4}{4}$$

8. What simple time signatures correspond to these compound time signatures:—

$$\frac{6}{16} \quad \frac{12}{16} \quad \frac{12}{8} \quad \frac{9}{4} \quad \frac{9}{8}$$

9. What is the rule about the use of the crotchet rest in $\frac{6}{8}$, $\frac{9}{8}$ or $\frac{12}{8}$ time?

10. Correct the following:—

11. Re-write this passage in $\frac{6}{8}$ time:—

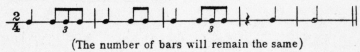

(The number of bars will remain the same)

12. What is a duplet, a quadruplet, a quintuplet? Give examples.

13. Group these quavers in two ways:—

(i) as in $\frac{3}{4}$ time
(ii) as in $\frac{6}{8}$ time.

14. Group these semiquavers: (a) in $\frac{3}{4}$ time; (b) in $\frac{6}{8}$ time; (c) in $\frac{12}{16}$ time:—

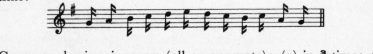

15. Group 24 demisemiquavers (all on one note): (a) in $\frac{3}{4}$ time; (b) in $\frac{6}{8}$ time; (c) in $\frac{12}{16}$ time; (d) in $\frac{3}{8}$ time (two bars).

16. Bar (add bar-lines) the following according to the time signature:—

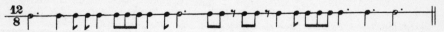

17. Supply time signature and bar-lines to the following:—

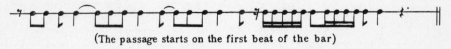

(The passage starts on the first beat of the bar)

EQUAL TEMPERAMENT – ENHARMONIC CHANGE DOUBLE SHARPS AND DOUBLE FLATS – MINOR SCALES – MELODIC MINOR – RELATIVE MAJOR AND RELATIVE MINOR – TONIC MAJOR AND TONIC MINOR – HARMONIC MINOR

109. The student will probably have noticed that the same black notes on the piano can be used for both sharps and flats and will probably be puzzled to know when to call a black note a sharp or a flat.

If a scale or key never needed more than two sharps or two flats, there would be no mystery: a black note would always be a *sharp* when used in a scale instead of a white note that was too *low* for the purpose required (e.g., F sharp instead of F in key G: a black note would always be a *flat* when used instead of a white note that was too *high* (e.g., B flat) instead of B in key F. Up to and including the key containing two sharps and the key containing two flats no black note is used first as a sharp and then as a flat. But when key signatures of three sharps and three flats are reached, we begin to find the same black note called a sharp in one key and a flat in another.

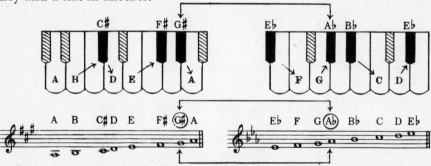

Referring to the above diagram, we observe that G sharp in the scale of A major is the same black note as A flat in the key of E flat major.

110. It would take too long to explain this fully. All the student need know is that the pianoforte and all keyboard instruments are deliberately " mistuned " in order to make one note do for two notes that are already very close together in pitch. In what is called **true or just intonation** (or tuning) G sharp and A flat would be at different pitches, though very close together, and the same would be true of C sharp and D flat.

111. **Temperament** is the term used to describe the tuning of a keyed instrument. **Equal temperament** is the term used to describe the now universally adopted system of *dividing the octave into twelve equal semitones*. This number of notes in the octave is convenient for the

fingers, but the greatest advantage of the system is that it provides complete freedom of **modulation** (i.e., changing from key to key). We can play G sharp as a note of the key of A major, then think of it as in the key of E flat major or in a key with more than three flats, and so modulate into a key far removed from the sharp key in which we started.

112.   This change of notation—or naming of notes—without altering their sound or pitch is called **enharmonic change.**   Two notes *with different letter names* represent *the same sound* and each is called the **enharmonic equivalent** of the other.   C sharp and D flat, D sharp and E flat, F sharp and G flat, G sharp and A flat, A sharp and B flat—each one of each couple of notes is the enharmonic equivalent of the other.

It must be emphasised that in true or just intonation *these pairs of notes would have different sounds although the difference in pitch would be very slight.*

113.   In **writing** scales we adhere to **true intonation.**
In **playing** keyboard scales we use **equal temperament.**
[E.g.—Though we might *read* a scale as C sharp major (seven sharps) we should play exactly the same keyboard notes as for the scale of D flat major (five flats).]

114.   A note may be raised *two-semitones*, viz., a whole tone, the result being called a **double sharp,** the sign for which is **×** (*not* ♯♯).

A note may also be lowered *two semitones*, the result being called a **double flat,** the sign for which is ♭♭.

A confusing feature of double sharps and double flats is that they are *white notes*, as shown in the following diagram:—

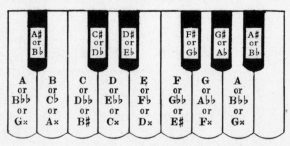

115.   To change from sharp to double sharp alter ♯ to **×** —see (a).
To change from flat   to double flat   alter ♭ to ♭♭—see (b).
To change from double sharp to sharp alter **×** to ♯ —see (c).
To change from double flat   to flat   alter ♭♭ to ♭ —see (d).

> N.B.—Formerly it was the custom, in changing back from double sharp to sharp and double flat to flat, to use both natural and sharp or flat: This custom has been observed in

music published up to quite modern times (See (cc) and (dd) below). There is now no need to follow this cumbersome procedure.

To change from double sharp or double flat to natural pitch use ♮. (See (e) and (f).)

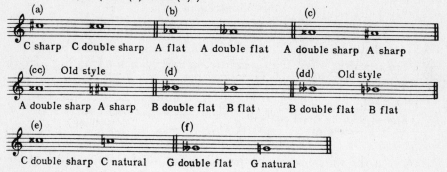

Minor Scales

116. The *major* scale is so-called because of its characteristic beginning with two tones (e.g., C to E), this distance or **interval** being known as a *major* or *bigger third*. (In solfa this distance or interval would be " doh " to " me." Intervals are explained in Chapter VIII.)

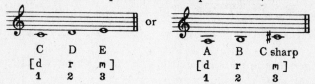

If instead of playing A to C sharp (major third) we play A to C natural:

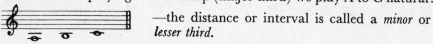

—the distance or interval is called a *minor* or *lesser third*.

On reference to the piano keyboard it will be found that
A major third consists of two tones or four semitones;
A minor third consists of one and a half tones or three semitones.
The scale beginning on A and using C natural is called the **minor scale** because of its use of the minor third.

117. The change from major to minor has a remarkable effect on the character or mood of the music: it is as if a shadow comes over the music. Although this analogy should not be carried too far, it is a fact that sadness is more easily associated with " minor " music than with " major "; there are, however, many jolly tunes in the minor. The terms " major *mode* " and " minor *mode* " are commonly used, the word *mode* approximating in meaning to *mood*.

118. Before the development of major and minor scales arrangements of notes called *modes* were used. If we play only on the *white* notes of the piano, say from D to D above, or from E to E above, or from F to F

above, etc., we produce modes. Of all the old modes (which possessed various names) two established themselves in modern music. They are:—

CDEFGABC formerly called *Ionian Mode* (now our Scale of C major), and

ABCDEFGA formerly called *Aeolian Mode* (the forerunner of our Minor Scale).

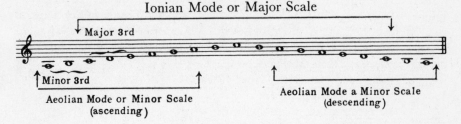

Ionian Mode or Major Scale

Aeolian Mode or Minor Scale (ascending)

Aeolian Mode a Minor Scale (descending)

119. In the minor scale the *descending form* of the old Aeolian Mode satisfied the ear and was left untouched.

The ascending form was felt to be unsatisfactory and needed modification. The last two notes ascending (G and A) sounded dull and unattractive. The *major* scale (ending on C) finished with a semitone, so why should not the *minor* scale (ending on A) do likewise? The G was therefore sharpened:—

But this left a difficult leap for the voice:—

Singers therefore improved matters by sharpening the F as well, so that the minor scale took this form:—

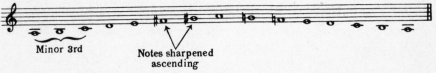

Minor 3rd

Notes sharpened ascending

The descending scale uses exactly the same notes as C major, except for beginning and ending on A.

120. The above scale would be known as that of A minor—*melodic form*, or simply as **A melodic minor,** because:—

(a) it starts and finishes on A;

(b) it starts with the characteristic minor third;

(c) it is designed to *suit the requirements of the human voice:* in other words it is *designed for melody.*

121. Because the C major scale and the A minor scale practically consist of the same notes, *they share the same key signature*—the artificial sharpening of F and G ascending *being ignored in the key signature.* If this seems puzzling, one should recall to mind *the exact resemblance of the descending form of both scales.*

As C major and A minor both use the same key signature (in spite of the constant use of accidentals in the latter scale) they are said to be **related.**

C major is called the **relative major** of A minor;
A minor is called the **relative minor** of C major.

122. It should be noted that A minor starts a minor 3rd below C major. This relationship holds good for all major and minor keys so related, and the general rule follows that *all minor keys take the key signature of the major scale a minor 3rd above*, or in other words *every minor scale takes the key signature of its relative major.*

Thus **every key signature stands for two keys—**

(a) a major key; and
(b) a minor key a minor third lower.

123. The following table shows all major and minor keys, with C major and A minor first as providing the pattern for all the rest:—

124. When a major scale and a minor scale start *on the same tonic*, they are described as **tonic major** and **tonic minor** respectively.

C major is the tonic major of C minor.

C minor is the tonic minor of C major.

The table in paragraph 123 shows that:—

whereas C major has no sharps or flats, C minor has three flats;

F major has one flat,   F minor has four flats;

B♭ major has two flats,   B♮ minor has five flats.

From this we obtain the rule that *the tonic minor always has three flats more in its key signature than has the tonic major.*

This rule is quite clear as applied to Key C and all the flat keys but can it be applied to the sharp keys?

(i) Referring once more to the table in paragraph 123, compare A major with A minor.

Whereas A major has three sharps, A minor has no sharps.   A minor has *three sharps less* than A major: this means that A minor is *three degrees flatter* than A major.   Relatively this is the same as saying that A minor has " three flats more," thus conforming to the rule already given.

(ii) Next, compare G major with G minor.

Whereas G major has one sharp, G minor has two flats.   This again amounts to the same thing as saying that G minor is *three degrees flatter* than G major—or that it has " three flats more."

If this seems difficult to understand, think of the problem mathematically, calling C major *zero* (no sharps or flats), the flats *minus* quantities and the sharps *plus* quantities:—

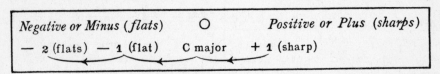

The distance from G major (1 sharp) to G minor (2 flats) is covered in 3 *moves* (shown by 3 curves) to the left, in the minus or flat direction.

G minor therefore is *three degrees flatter* than G major, which is the same as saying that G minor has *three flats more.*

(iii) D major has two sharps, D minor one flat—once again involving *three* moves in the flat direction.

(iv) B major has five sharps, B minor two sharps, that is, three sharps less, B minor being *three degrees flatter* than B major.

The rule is best put in this form:—

The tonic minor always has 3 flats more or 3 sharps less (or their equivalent) than the tonic major;

The tonic major always has 3 sharps more or 3 flats less (or their equivalent) than the tonic minor.

125. The arrangement of tones and semitones in the melodic minor scale is different from that in the major scale.

Ascending —the semitones occur between 2 and 3, and 7 and 8—
the pattern being TONE – SEMITONE – TONE – TONE –
TONE – TONE – SEMITONE.

Descending—the semitones occur between 6 and 5, and 3 and 2—
the pattern (downwards) being TONE – TONE – SEMI-
TONE – TONE – TONE – SEMITONE – TONE.

N.B.—In the above the notes forming the semitones are placed close together as well as being joined by a slur.

126.   In melodic minor scales of five sharps or more *double sharps* occur. It will be remembered that the 6th and 7th degrees of the ascending melodic minor scale are always sharpened against the key signature.   If these degrees are already sharpened notes, further sharpening makes them double sharps.

In G sharp minor (five sharps signature) and D sharp minor (six sharps signature) the seventh degree ascending will be a double sharp: while in A sharp minor (seven sharps signature) both the sixth and the seventh degrees ascending will be double sharps:—

G sharp melodic minor

D sharp melodic minor

A sharp melodic minor

127.   The remaining melodic minor scales are given below (A minor, G sharp minor, D sharp minor and A sharp minor have already been shown).   As a change the bass clef is used:—

Sharp Keys

E melodic minor

B melodic minor

F sharp melodic minor

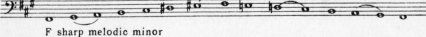

C sharp melodic minor

Flat Keys

D melodic minor

G melodic minor

C melodic minor

F melodic minor

B flat melodic minor

E flat melodic minor

A flat melodic minor

N.B.— (i) In key D minor (above) the sixth degree, being B *flat*, according to key signature, is sharpened by being changed to B *natural*.

    (ii) In key G minor the sixth degree, being E flat, according to the key signature, is sharpened by being changed to E *natural*.

  (iii) In all the other flat melodic minor scales both sixth and seventh degrees being flat, according to the key signature, are sharpened by being changed to naturals.

128.   There is still one other kind of minor scale—the **harmonic minor.** This is so-called because it is important *harmonically*—that is, it is employed in constructing *chords* in the minor key. In this type of scale only the seventh degree contradicts the key signature, and the scale is *the same ascending and descending*.

All the harmonic minors are given below on both staves, but only A minor is given in both ascending and descending aspects.

Harmonic Minor Scales

A harmonic minor

Sharp Keys

Flat Keys

It will be noticed that there is in the harmonic minor scale an awkward leap between the sixth and seventh degrees (called an *augmented 2nd*—explained in paragraph 135) which is avoided in the melodic minor scale for the sake of voices. Really, however, vocal music (music for voices) nowadays makes use of all sorts of awkward progressions formerly thought to be unvocal. There are *three semitones* in the harmonic minor scale between 2 and 3, 5 and 6, and 7 and 8.

129. The same key signature is used for both melodic and harmonic forms of any particular minor scale. The technical names (tonic, supertonic mediant, etc.) are applied to the degrees of the minor scale as with the major scale, but it should be noticed that there is *no leading note* in the *descending* form of the melodic minor scale. The seventh note will be called the " leading note " in the ascending form, but merely the seventh degree in the descending form. The submediant (sixth degree) of the same type of scale varies according to whether the scale is ascending or descending. Thus in C melodic minor the submediant is A natural ascending and A flat descending.

130. In paragraphs 83 and 85 the major scales were written without key signatures. When minor scales are so written, great care is needed with the accidentals, but at the same time the absence of key signatures will mean that accidentals which would have contradicted the key signatures may be omitted. The rule that accidentals hold good throughout a bar cannot be applied when scales are written without bar-lines. Each note must be dealt with separately:—

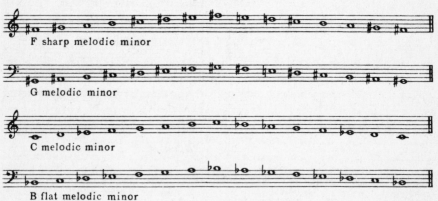

F sharp melodic minor

G melodic minor

C melodic minor

B flat melodic minor

131. As with major scales (See paragraph 93) examination questions sometimes ask for minor scales to begin and end on a note other than the tonic.

Example (i)

Write the harmonic minor scale of B flat beginning and ending on the mediant (a) without key signature; (b) with key signature.

Method of Working

The mediant is D flat: the scale starts on this note.

Answer

(a)

(b)

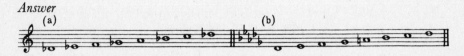

Example (ii)

Write the melodic minor scale of G sharp, beginning and ending on the submediant (a) without key signature; (b) with key signature.

Method of Working

In this " extreme " sort of question bear in mind that the submediant *ascending* is E sharp and the submediant descending is E natural, so that the two forms of the melodic minor must be separated.

Answer

(a)

(b)

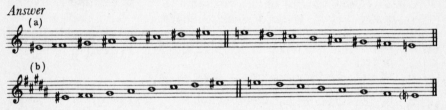

QUESTIONS AND EXERCISES ON CHAPTER VII

1. What is meant by: (a) Temperament?
   (b) Equal Temperament?

2. What is meant by: (a) Enharmonic Change?
   (b) Enharmonic Equivalent?

3. (a) What do we call the result of raising a note by two semitones?
   (b) Write the sign used to obtain this result.
   (c) What do we call the result of lowering a note by two semitones?
   (d) Write the sign used to obtain this result.

4. What other names can be given to these notes on the piano keyboard: A sharp, C, D flat, E, F sharp, G, F double sharp, E double flat?

5. Name these notes, and then give the enharmonic equivalents of the notes (a), (b), (c), (d), (e):—

(a)   (b)   (c)   (d)   (e)

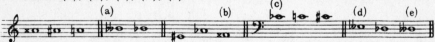

6. Why is the minor scale so called?

7. From what " mode " is the minor scale derived?

8. (a) In what respect does the melodic minor scale contradict its key signature?
   (b) What difference in pitch separates the tonic of a major scale from the tonic of its relative minor?

9. Write the key signatures, on both staves bracketed together, of these minor scales:—B, C, D, E, F, G, A, A flat.

10. What is the difference between a tonic minor and a relative minor?

11. Between which degrees of the melodic minor scale do semitones occur: (a) ascending; (b) descending?

12. Write these melodic minor scales with key signatures on both staves bracketed—one octave ascending and descending. Mark the semitones:—C, B, B flat, C sharp, G sharp.

13. Write these melodic minor scales without key signatures on both staves bracketed—one octave ascending and descending. Use minims, being careful of the direction of the stems, and mark the semitones:—G, F, E flat, F sharp, A sharp.

14. (a) Between which degrees of the harmonic minor scale do semitones occur?
(b) Why is the harmonic minor scale so called?

15. Write the following harmonic minor scales on the treble stave, one octave ascending, with key signatures. Use crotchets, being careful of the direction of the stems, and mark the semitones with slurs:—
A, D, E, D sharp, A flat.

16. Write in semibreves, one octave, ascending and descending of each of the following scales, using key signatures and marking the semitones:—
G harmonic minor (treble clef) beginning and ending on the leading note;
B melodic minor (bass clef) beginning and ending on the mediant;
C harmonic minor (treble clef) beginning and ending on the subdominant;
F sharp melodic minor (bass clef) beginning and ending on the dominant;
F harmonic minor (treble clef) beginning and ending on the submediant.

17. None of the following scales begins on the tonic. Name the scale in each case and state the degree of the scale on which each starts:—

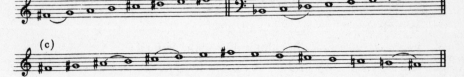

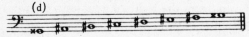

18. Write with key signatures, one octave ascending and descending, the following scales grouped according to the time signatures. Insert bar-lines and complete the second bar with rests, properly arranged, as required:—

    (a) A harmonic minor in quavers, in $\frac{4}{4}$ time;

    (b) C sharp melodic minor in semiquavers, in $\frac{6}{8}$ time;

    (c) B flat harmonic minor in demisemiquavers, in $\frac{3}{8}$ time.

19. Complete the following scales by adding sharps and flats where required. Omit key signatures.

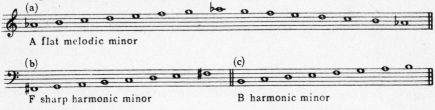

A flat melodic minor

F sharp harmonic minor   B harmonic minor

20. Add key signatures to the following:—

67

CHAPTER VIII

DIATONIC INTERVALS

132. The word **interval** has already been used in paragraphs 66 and 116. It is defined as the *difference in pitch* between two sounds. Put in a different way an interval may be described as the *vertical distance* between two sounds.

We attach the idea of *space* to the word as used in its normal sense. If there are *three* posts in a line, there would be *two* spaces or intervals, the number of intervals being always one less than the number of posts or points. Applying this to music one would expect that intervals would be measured thus:— C D E

From C to E—*two* intervals or spaces.

But this is not the case in musical theory, in which *The naming of an interval depends upon the number of letter-names involved*, and not upon the number of spaces.

C D E involves *three* letter-names of notes, and the interval C to E is called a *third*—illogical as this may seem.

Whatever the sharps or flats placed before C and E *the interval will be called a third of some kind*.

In a note to paragraph 62 and again in paragraph 116 the *major third* and *minor third* are referred to: C to E as a major third and A to C as a minor third, C to E flat would also be a minor third.

Again in paragraph 65 the distance in pitch from C to D is called a *tone*: it could equally well be called a **second** of some kind, and the semitone distance (E to F in the scale of C) would also be a *second* of another kind, because in both cases *two* different letter-names are concerned.

133. The **quality** of an interval depends upon *the number of semitones* in it. A major interval has a *different quality* from that of a minor interval.

> The interval C to E is a major third (or has a major quality) because it contains 4 semitones (C to C sharp, C sharp to D, D to D sharp, D sharp to E).
>
> The interval C to E flat is a minor third (or has a minor quality) because it contains 3 semitones.
>
> The interval C to D is a major second because it contains 2 semitones.
>
> The interval C to D flat is a minor second because it contains 1 semitone.

Various words are used to describe the *quality* of an interval, quite apart from its *numerical* description. They are:—

> (a) major and minor;
> (b) augmented and diminished;
> (c) perfect.

134. The major scale is the standard of measurement for the quality and numerical description of intervals:—

Major 2nd   Major 3rd   Perfect 4th   Perfect 5th

Major 6th   Major 7th   Perfect Octave
                              or 8th

When two parts or voices have the same note, they are said to be in **unison** (one sound). Although there is in this case *no real interval*, yet the unison is called *perfect*, just as the octave is so called:—

Perfect Unison
(or 1st)

N.B.—The term **major** is applied to **2nds, 3rds, 6ths** and **7ths.**
The term **perfect** is applied to **1sts** (**Unisons**), **4ths, 5ths** and **8ths** (**Octaves**).

Any major scale may be used for illustration:—

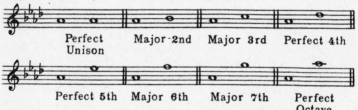

Perfect   Major 2nd   Major 3rd   Perfect 4th
Unison

Perfect 5th   Major 6th   Major 7th   Perfect
                                          Octave

135. There are **four qualities of major intervals;**
and **three qualities of perfect intervals.**

A **major** interval . . .   may be increased to **augmented**
(by the addition of one semitone)
may be decreased to **minor**
(by the loss of one semitone)
may be further decreased to **diminished**
(by the loss of two semitones)

A **perfect** interval . . .   may be increased to **augmented**
(by the addition of one semitone)
may be decreased to **diminished**
(by the loss of one semitone)

Thus: *perfect* intervals never become minor: they reduce to *diminished* only.

Major and Minor 3rds and 6ths ⎫ are called **concordant intervals**
Perfect 4ths, 5ths and Octaves ⎬   or **concords**
All 2nds and 7ths and Augmented ⎫ are called **discordant intervals**
and Diminished Intervals ⎬   or **discords**

69

N.B.—It must not be supposed that " discordant " means necessarily ugly or unpleasant. The richest and most beautiful harmonic effects in music are obtained by the use of discords.

A concordant interval (or concord) is complete in effect, and needs nothing else to follow it.

A discordant interval (or discord) is incomplete in effect, and needs some other chord to follow it, this being called its " resolution."

136. With the tonic of a major scale as the lower note of an interval only *major* and *perfect* intervals are produced.

Other intervals are produced when the lower note is a note *other than the tonic*, as shown below.

In the first line of intervals below, the notes of each interval are shown one after the other, as in a melody.   They are therefore said to be shown as **melodic intervals.**

In the second line below, the notes of each interval are shown as sounded together as in harmony.   They are therefore said to be shown as **harmonic intervals.**

More intervals in the Key of C (shown as *melodic* intervals)

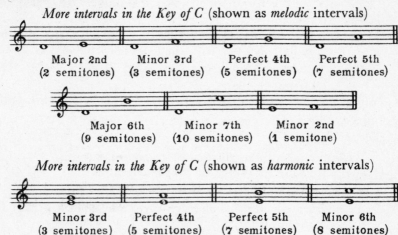

More intervals in the Key of C (shown as *harmonic* intervals)

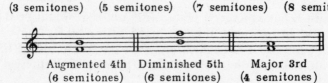

Intervals in the Key of A minor

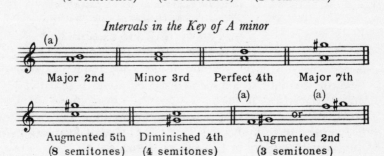

(The intervals marked " a " are harmonic intervals, not melodic. It is impossible to write the interval of a second with one note directly above the other.)

The intervals in all the other major and minor scales may be found in similar fashion to the above.

137. **How to find the note making a specified interval above a given note:—**

(1) To find the note making *a major or perfect interval* above a given note, *treat the given note as the tonic* and pitch the required note from it.

Example (i)

Which note is a perfect fourth above F?

Answer

The 4th note up from F in the scale of F major, that is *B flat*.

$$\begin{bmatrix} - & F & G & A & B\,flat— \\ - & 1 & 2 & 3 & 4 & — \end{bmatrix}$$

Example (ii)

Which note is a major seventh above D flat?

Answer

The 7th note up from D flat in the scale of D flat major, that is, *C*.

D flat	E flat	F	G flat	A flat	B flat	C
1	2	3	4	5	6	7

(2) To find the note making *a minor, augmented or diminished interval* above a given note.

Example (i)

Write the note an augmented fifth above E flat.

Method of Working

A fifth is a perfect interval.

An augmented fifth has one more semitone than a perfect fifth (See paragraph 135).

With E flat as tonic, a perfect fifth above it would be B flat, this note being found in E flat major scale.

An augmented fifth, therefore, above E flat would be B natural, thus adding one more semitone to the perfect interval.

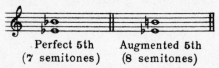

    Perfect 5th   Augmented 5th
   (7 semitones)   (8 semitones)

Example (ii)

Write the note an augmented second above F sharp.

Method of Working

An augmented second has one more semitone than a major 2nd.

A major second above F sharp is G sharp, this note being the second note up in F sharp major scale.

71

An augmented second about F sharp will therefore be G double sharp.

Major 2nd   Augmented 2nd
(2 semitones)   (3 semitones)

Note that, however big the interval of the second above F sharp, the upper note must be G " something " or the interval will cease to be a second.   G double sharp is the same note as A natural on the keyboard, but, if A natural were substituted for G double sharp, the interval would then be a minor third.

138.   **How to find the note making a specified interval below a given note:—**

In such cases the best method is to count down the given distance (second, third, etc.), ignoring sharps and flats, then begin by treating the lower note as the tonic of a scale.   It will be necessary to adjust the *lower* note this time to secure the required " quality " of interval (major, minor, perfect, augmented or diminished).

Example (i)

A perfect fifth below A flat?

Method of Working

Counting downwards we reach D as a fifth of some kind below A. Write A and D without sharps or flats:—

This interval is a perfect fifth, because A is the fifth note up in the major scale of D.

The given note, however, is A flat.   If we retain D natural, the interval will be a semitone less than a perfect fifth below A flat.

We therefore flatten the D to obtain the required perfect fifth:—

Perfect 5th
below A flat

Example (ii)

A minor seventh below C sharp?

Method of Working

D is the seventh note down from C

In the scale of D major, *C sharp* would give a *major* seventh.   To produce a *minor* seventh all we have to do is to sharpen D, thus lessening the seventh by a semitone.

Minor 7th   Major 7th   Minor 7th

Example (iii)

A minor sixth below A sharp?

Method of Working

C is the sixth note down from A

In the scale of C major, A would give the major sixth.
If we sharpen *both* notes, we shall still have a major sixth:—

Major 6th

The interval must be reduced by one semitone to produce a minor sixth. The top note, A sharp, cannot be lowered because it is the given note. The C sharp is therefore raised in order to reduce the size of the interval.

Minor 6th

139. In paragraph 78 it was stated that major and minor scales are called diatonic, because they proceed mainly through tones.

As all the intervals dealt with in this chapter are to be found in major and minor scales, they are called **diatonic intervals**, because they are found only in diatonic (major and minor) scales.

QUESTIONS AND EXERCISES ON CHAPTER VIII

1. (a) What is an interval.
    (b) On what principle are intervals named?

2. What words are used to describe the *quality* of intervals apart from their numerical description?

3. (a) Which intervals are never described as major?
    (b) How are these intervals described?

4. (a) What other name can be given to a semitone?
    (b) What is meant by saying that voices or parts are in unison?
    (c) How many semitones are there in: (i) a major 3rd; (ii) a perfect 4th; (iii) augmented 5th; (iv) a minor 7th?

5. (a) By how many semitones can a major interval: (i) be increased;
                                                  (ii) be decreased?
    (b) By how many semitones can a perfect interval: (i) be increased;
                                                     (ii) be decreased?

6. (a) What is the difference between a concordant interval and a discordant interval?
    (b) What is the difference between a melodic interval and a harmonic interval?

7. Name these intervals:—

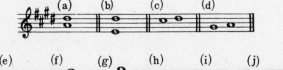

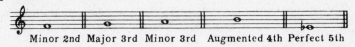

8. Write above these given notes the notes that form the intervals specified:—

Minor 2nd   Major 3rd   Minor 3rd   Augmented 4th   Perfect 5th

Minor 6th   Major 6th   Minor 7th   Major 7th   Diminished 4th   Augmented 5th

9. Name these intervals and state which are concordant and which discordant:—

10. In the following the intervals are shown as occurring in a musical passage. What general term would be applied to such intervals? Name them individually by referring to their letter names.

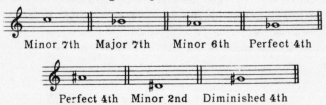

11. Write the notes forming the specified intervals below these notes:—

Minor 7th   Major 7th   Minor 6th   Perfect 4th

Perfect 4th   Minor 2nd   Diminished 4th

12. What are diatonic intervals?

CHAPTER IX

THE CHROMATIC AND OTHER SCALES – CHROMATIC INTERVALS – INVERSION OF INTERVALS – COMPOUND INTERVALS

140. There are other scales besides the *diatonic* major and minor scales (in which seven differently named notes make up each scale). The most important of these other scales is that which proceeds **entirely through semitones** (twelve different notes making up the scale). This is the **chromatic scale,** and it can be produced by beginning on middle C and playing every note, black and white, until the C above is reached.

Though it may be difficult to think of *colour* in connection with music, yet there is such a thing as *tone colour*, the tone colour of a violin, for instance, being easily distinguished from that of a trumpet.

The word **chromatic** means **coloured**, and the chromatic scale is so-called because it is said to have more " colour " than the diatonic scales. Musical experience only will show how true this is; the beginner must take this statement for granted.

Whatever the starting note for a chromatic scale it will always sound the same (allowing for the difference in pitch of the starting note); hence *it lacks character* and the ear soon tires of it.

141. *In diatonic scales no alphabetical pitch name is ever repeated*, each being used once only in each octave.

In chromatic scales alphabetical pitch names are repeated, but with different accidentals.

142. There are two ways of writing chromatic scales:—
      (a) the **harmonic,**
and (b) the **melodic**
though composers often write them in any way they fancy. The *melodic* way is in many respects the easier, but the *harmonic* is most frequently asked for in examinations.

143. **The harmonic chromatic scale** is obtained thus:—
With C as tonic
      (a) Write the notes of the C major scale with *the tones* well spaced:

      (b) Add those notes *from both forms of the minor scale* which differ from those of the major scale: some natural signs will need to be added to contradict the flats:—

(c) Add a flattened second degree and sharpened fourth degree:

This would be called *the harmonic chromatic scale of C* written without key signature.   It is *the same ascending and descending.*

N.B.—In both forms of the chromatic scale *the fourth is always sharpened* ascending and descending.

144.   In practice, however, chromatic scales are written with the major or minor key signature of the tonic on which they begin.

Examples

(a) *Using the major key signature of D flat.*

Write D flat major scale, then add flattened 2nd, 3rd, 6th and 7th degrees, and a sharpened 4th:

4th Sharpened

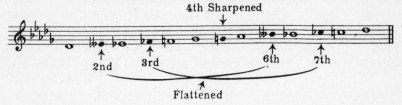

2nd   3rd   6th   7th

Flattened

In descending there will be the same notes with accidentals modified according to the order of the notes:

4th Sharpened

The harmonic chromatic scale beginning on D flat and written with the major key signature would therefore appear as follows:

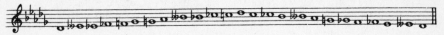

(b) *Using the minor key signature of C sharp.*

Write C sharp minor scale *without accidentals*, then add flattened 2nd degree and sharpened 3rd, 4th, 6th and 7th degrees:

N.B.—In the above the semibreves represent the notes of C sharp minor scale.

145.   It will be noticed that in the harmonic chromatic scale of D flat the *sharpened* fourth is G *natural*, the *flattened* second is E *double* flat, and the *flattened* sixth is B *double* flat: while in the harmonic chromatic scale of C sharp the *flattened* second is D *natural*, and the *sharpened* fourth is F *double* sharp.

Before going further the student should refer again to paragraphs 114, 115, and particularly paragraph 124 which deals with movement in a flat or sharp direction. If a sharp is to be flattened, it becomes a natural: if a flat is to be sharpened, it becomes a natural. Double sharps and double flats are explained in paragraphs 114 and 115.

146. In checking the correctness of harmonic chromatic scales *with key signatures* it should be remembered that:—

> *With a major signature* there should be 9 accidentals ascending and 6 descending;
>
> *With a minor signature* there should be 6 accidentals ascending and 9 descending.

147. **The melodic chromatic scale** differs from the harmonic form only in its *ascending* form. It needs fewer accidentals and is therefore easier to read:—

(a) *Without key signature*, sharpen 1st, 2nd, 4th and 6th degrees:

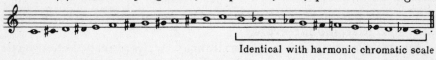

Identical with harmonic chromatic scale

(b) *With major key signature*, write the major scale and then sharpen each degree except 3rd and 7th:

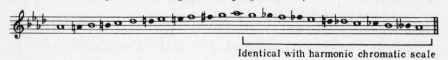

Identical with harmonic chromatic scale

(c) *With minor key signature*, write the minor scale without accidentals and then sharpen each degree except 2nd and 5th:

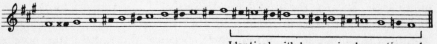

Identical with harmonic chromatic scale

> *Note*. Students familiar with tonic solfa will easily memorise the melodic chromatic scale as;—
>
> d de r re m f fe s se l le te d't ta l la s fe f m ma r ra d

148. This notation may seem needlessly complicated, but the reason for the notation of the harmonic chromatic scale really becomes clear only when chromatic harmony is studied: the notation of the melodic chromatic scale is designed to facilitate reading of melody.

149. In addition to the kinds of scales already mentioned there are others such as the **whole tone scale,** the **pentatonic scale** and a melodic minor scale the same ascending and descending. Composers may also decide on a scale of their own devising in order to produce special melodic and harmonic effects.

(a) The whole tone scale consisting entirely of tones, having no semitones:

1   2   3   4   5   6 ⟶ All tones

(b) The pentatonic—or " five note " scale, which can be produced by playing only on the black notes of the piano keyboard:

(Black notes)   Transposed to key C

(c) A melodic minor the same ascending and descending:

150. In paragraph 139 intervals to be found only in diatonic scales are called **diatonic intervals.**

Similarly intervals found only in chromatic scales are called **chromatic intervals.**

Chromatic intervals include the **chromatic semitone**, and the **diminished octave**, the **augmented third** and the **diminished 6th**, the **diminished third** and the **augmented sixth.**

151.   (i) **The chromatic semitone** and **the diminished octave:—**

This chromatic semitone could not possibly belong to any major or minor scale, because the alphabetical name of a note is never found more than once in the same diatonic scale (See paragraph 141). Although a semitone, it cannot be a minor *second*, because the same letter note is repeated. It will be described as an **augmented unison** (See paragraph 134).

If the G sharp remains where it is and the G natural is placed an octave higher, the resulting interval would be called a **diminished octave:—**

Once again no major or minor scale could at one and the same time contain the note G and itself sharped.

(ii) **The augmented third** and **the diminished sixth:—**

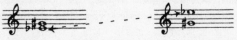

These two intervals can be found only in a chromatic scale:

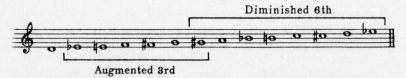

Diminished 6th

Augmented 3rd

(iii) **The diminished third and the augmented sixth:—**

These two intervals can be found only in a chromatic scale:

Augmented 6th

Diminished 3rd

152.   Raising the lower note of an interval by an octave and so putting it above the other note (as was done with the lower notes of the augmented unison, augmented third and diminished third in paragraph 151), or lowering the upper note of an interval by an octave and so putting it below the other note is called **inverting** an interval (or turning it upside-down).   When an interval is inverted, the new arrangement brought about is called an **inversion**:—

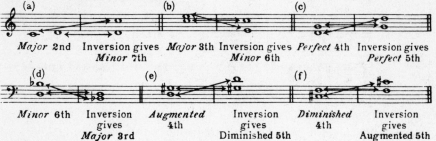

Major 2nd   Inversion gives   *Major* 3th   Inversion gives   *Perfect* 4th   Inversion gives
　　　　　Minor 7th　　　　　*Minor* 6th　　　　　*Perfect* 5th

Minor 6th   Inversion   *Augmented*   Inversion   *Diminished*   Inversion
　gives　　　 4th　　　 gives　　　 4th　　　 gives
Major 3rd　　　　　Diminished 5th　　　　Augmented 5th

Rule for calculating inversions:—

> *Subtract the number of the given interval from 9, and the number of the inversion will be the answer.*

Referring to the above examples:—

    (a) To invert a 2nd: 2 from 9 leaves 7.   The inversion is a 7th.
    (b) To invert a 3rd: 3 from 9 leaves 6.   The inversion is a 6th.
    (c) To invert a 4th: 4 from 9 leaves 5.   The inversion is a 5th.
                   And so on.

Inversion also brings about another change.   Referring to the above examples:—

    (a) – (b) Major intervals when inverted become minor.
    (d)   Minor intervals when inverted become major.
    (e) Augmented intervals when inverted become diminished.
    (f) Diminished intervals when inverted become augmented.
                    but
    (c) Perfect intervals when inverted remain perfect.

Table of Intervals.

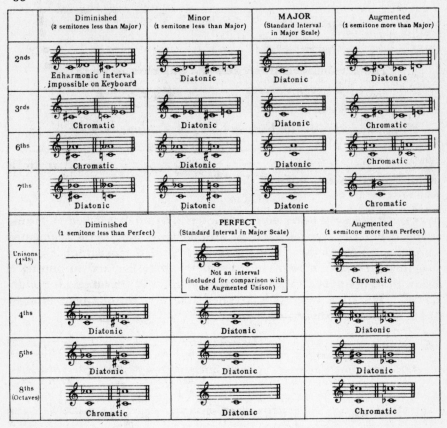

	Diminished (2 semitones less than Major)	Minor (1 semitone less than Major)	MAJOR (Standard Interval in Major Scale)	Augmented (1 semitone more than Major)
2nds	Enharmonic interval impossible on Keyboard	Diatonic	Diatonic	Diatonic
3rds	Chromatic	Diatonic	Diatonic	Chromatic
6ths	Chromatic	Diatonic	Diatonic	Chromatic
7ths	Diatonic	Diatonic	Diatonic	Chromatic

	Diminished (1 semitone less than Perfect)	PERFECT (Standard Interval in Major Scale)	Augmented (1 semitone more than Perfect)
Unisons (1sts)	—	Not an interval (included for comparison with the Augmented Unison)	Chromatic
4ths	Diatonic	Diatonic	Diatonic
5ths	Diatonic	Diatonic	Diatonic
8ths (Octaves)	Chromatic	Diatonic	Chromatic

154. An interval may be reduced in size either by raising the lower note a *chromatic* semitone (or two semitones in some cases) or by lowering the higher note a chromatic semitone (or two semitones). The semitones must be chromatic because the changed note must retain the same alphabetical name as the original note: to reduce an interval by a diatonic semitone would involve the use of a different alphabetical name and a change in the numerical description of the interval. An interval will retain its numerical description no matter to what extent it is reduced or enlarged by *chromatic semitones*.

Example

D to B will be a sixth of some kind irrespective of accidentals placed before either or both notes:—

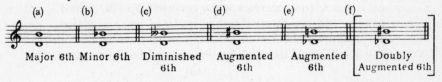

(a)	(b)	(c)	(d)	(e)	(f)
Major 6th	Minor 6th	Diminished 6th	Augmented 6th	Augmented 6th	Doubly Augmented 6th

(f) is an "invented" interval and quite impracticable.

If (d) were written 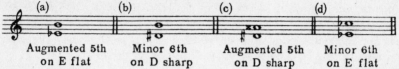 it would cease to be a sixth.

155. *Enharmonic change* (explained in paragraph 112) enters very largely into the nomenclature of intervals.

The following examples all use the same two notes on the piano keyboard but they all have different notation:—

(a)	(b)	(c)	(d)
Augmented 5th on E flat	Minor 6th on D sharp	Augmented 5th on D sharp	Minor 6th on E flat

Although utilising the same two keyboard notes (a) and (c) would be called discords (See paragraph 135), while (b) and (d) would be called concords. The explanation of these anomalies will be found in Chapter VII on Equal Temperament: the harmonic context in which the intervals are used will also help us to distinguish between concords and discords.

156. Sometimes in examinations candidates are asked to state all the keys in which a given interval may occur. Most intervals occur in more than one key.

Example (a)

State all the keys in which this interval may be found:—

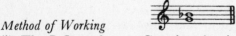

Method of Working
(i) Since D sharp is one of the notes, the interval cannot occur in any *major* key containing less than 4 sharps. The major keys concerned will therefore be E, B, F sharp and C sharp, with their relative minors C sharp (but not G sharp minor because F double sharp is the leading note), D sharp and A sharp.
(ii) D sharp is also the leading note of E minor.
Complete list: E minor, E major, C sharp minor, B major, F sharp major, D sharp minor, C sharp major and A sharp minor.
N.B.—In this type of question the *harmonic* minor is usually taken as the standard minor key pattern, with its minor sixth above the tonic and its sharpened leading note, and not the melodic minor.

Example (b)

State all the keys in which this interval may be found:—

Method of Working
(i) The B flat rules out C major, A minor and all sharp keys.
(ii) All flat major keys will be included up to 4 flats. The G natural rules out D flat major.
(iii) The relative minors of the above flat keys will be included except C minor, which has B natural for its leading note.
Complete list: F major, D minor, B flat major, G minor, E flat major, A flat major and F minor.

157.   Intervals containing a sharp and a flat such as
may puzzle the student who is asked to state the keys in
which such an interval may be found. *There is of course no key signature
containing both sharps and flats,* but a number of harmonic minor scales
have a flat key signature with a sharpened leading note contradicting
the signature. In such a case as the interval quoted we apply *the rule of
the sharper note,* which is to the effect that *the sharper note will be the leading
note of the scale.*

In the interval under consideration F sharp is obviously the sharper
note, and this as leading note gives G minor as the key.

158.   Double sharps are obviously sharper notes than sharps. They
occur in minor keys only as leading notes (we are dealing only with
harmonic minor scales), and no major scale contains double sharps or
double flats.

This interval can occur only in D sharp minor, the

C double sharp being the leading note.

159.   When it is not at once apparent which of two notes is the sharper,
as in this interval (in which both notes are sharps) :—

imagine them each in turn as a tonic.

G as tonic has one sharp, G sharp as tonic would have 8 sharps.
B as tonic has five sharps, B sharp as tonic would have 12 sharps.
B sharp is therefore the sharper note.

Explanation

If we sharpen a note, 7 sharps are added to its key signature when
considered as a tonic.

Thus C major has no sharps:
But C sharp major has 7 sharps (0 plus 7 = 7).
G major has one sharp:

G sharp major has 1 plus 7 sharps = 8
B major has five sharps:
B sharp major has 5 plus 7 sharps = 12.
There are of course no such keys as G sharp major and B sharp
major, but by *imagining* such keys we apply the rule of the
sharper note.

160.   When an interval consists of a natural and a flattened note, the
natural is of course the sharper note.

In   B is the sharper note, and is the leading note, the

key being C minor.

161. Examination questions sometimes require that one note of a given interval should be changed enharmonically and the resulting interval given its new name. Commonsense should be exercised in choosing which note is to be given its enharmonic equivalent.

Thus in changing the following interval

This change is better than

Diminished 7th   Doubly Augmented 5th
(an impracticable interval)

162. **More suggestions in naming intervals:—**

Suppose is to be named.

(i) E to A (EFGA) is a 4th of some kind.
(ii) Consider the lower note as the tonic of E major.
(iii) E to A natural would be a perfect 4th.
(iv) E to A flat is a semitone less than a perfect 4th, and is therefore a *diminished* 4th.

163. In the case of

(i) This is a 3rd (ABC) of some kind.
(ii) Considering A sharp as tonic would be too complicated, as key A sharp would have 10 sharps (A has 3; A sharp would have 3 plus 7 = 10.)
(iii) If the lower note cannot be a convenient tonic, lower or raise it one chromatic semitone (keep the same alphabetical name). In this case lower it to become A natural.
(iv) In the scale of A major, A to C sharp is a major third.
(v) In the given interval both A and C sharp are sharpened, A becoming A sharp and C sharp becoming C double sharp: both being raised a semitone they keep their relative positions and the interval remains unchanged as a major 3rd.

164. The above is the best way of measuring intervals—viz., by reference to the standard intervals of the major scale with the lower note considered as the tonic. Intervals can however be measured by the number of semitones making up the intervals. A table of measurements is given below:—

    1 semitone   = minor 2nd (or augmented unison)
    2 semitones = major 2nd or diminished 3rd
    3 semitones = augmented 2nd or minor 3rd
    4 semitones = major 3rd or diminished 4th
    5 semitones = augmented 3rd or perfect 4th
    6 semitones = augmented 4th or diminished 5th
    7 semitones = perfect 5th or diminished 6th

8 semitones = augmented 5th or minor 6th
9 semitones = major 6th or diminished 7th
10 semitones = augmented 6th or minor 7th
11 semitones = major 7th or diminished 8ve
12 semitones = augmented 7th or perfect 8ve.

165. Intervals are also classified as **simple** and **compound.**
A *simple interval* does not exceed the compass of an octave.
A *compound interval* is greater than an octave.
The following are examples of compound intervals:—

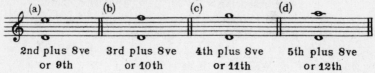

| 2nd plus 8ve | 3rd plus 8ve | 4th plus 8ve | 5th plus 8ve |
| or 9th | or 10th | or 11th | or 12th |

To find the name of a compound interval add 7 to the number of the simple interval:

(a) $2 + 7 = 9$; (b) $3 + 7 = 10$; (c) $4 + 7 = 11$; (d) $5 + 7 = 12$.
A compound 2nd is a 9th
A compound 3rd is a 10th
A compound 4th is an 11th
A compound 5th is a 12th
A compound 6th is a 13th
A compound 7th is a 14th
A compound 8ve is a 15th.

166. In **inverting compound intervals** it will be insufficient to raise or lower one of the notes by *one* octave, because the relative positions of the two notes would be unchanged, the higher still being the higher, and the lower still being the lower. It is necessary to raise or lower one note by *two* octaves:—

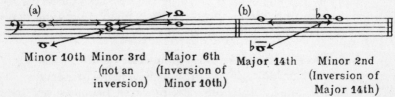

| Minor 10th | Minor 3rd (not an inversion) | Major 6th (Inversion of Minor 10th) | Major 14th | Minor 2nd (Inversion of Major 14th) |

An alternative method is to *raise* the *lower* note by *one* octave, and to *lower* the *upper* note by *one* octave.
Using the same intervals as above:—

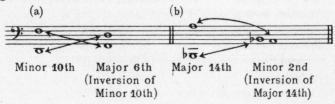

| Minor 10th | Major 6th (Inversion of Minor 10th) | Major 14th | Minor 2nd (Inversion of Major 14th) |

QUESTIONS AND EXERCISES ON CHAPTER IX

1. What is the meaning of the word " chromatic " ?
2. What is the difference between diatonic and chromatic scales as regards—
   (a) the occurrence of semitones;
   (b) the use of alphabetical pitch names?
3. How is the harmonic chromatic scale constructed
   (a) without key signature;
   (b) with a major key signature?
4. Write the harmonic chromatic scales beginning on D and E flat
   (a) without key signature;
   (b) with major key signatures; } (treble stave only)
   (c) with minor key signatures.
5. Write the melodic chromatic scales beginning on E and G (ascending forms only)
   (a) without key signature;
   (b) with major key signatures; } (bass stave only)
   (c) with minor key signatures.
6. Write
   (a) the whole tone scale beginning on D (ascending only);
   (b) the pentatonic scale beginning on F (ascending only).
7. Name these intervals and mark those that are diatonic with " D," and those that are chromatic with " C ":—

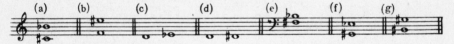

8. Write the following intervals:—
   On the treble stave
   > (a) perfect 4th above E; (b) diminished 7th above D; (c) chromatic semitone above G: (d) diminished 6th above A sharp.

   On the bass stave
   > (a) major 3rd below C; (b) diminished 5th below E flat; (c) major 6th below B: (d) augmented 8ve below C sharp.
9. (a) What is meant by inverting an interval?
   (b) What is the rule for calculating the numerical description of the inversion of an interval?
10. What do major   intervals become when inverted?
    What do minor   intervals become when inverted?
    What do augmented intervals become when inverted?
    What do diminished intervals become when inverted?
    What do perfect   intervals become when inverted?
11. (a) What is a compound interval?
    (b) Give the rule for calculating the numerical description of a

compound interval given the name of the corresponding simple interval.

(c) What is the difference between a harmonic interval and a melodic interval?

12. Name each of these intervals, then invert them in turn and name the inversions:—

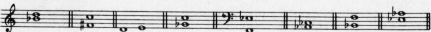

13. Name each of these intervals, then invert them in turn and name the inversions:—

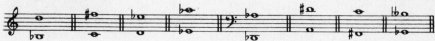

14. Enharmonically change one of the notes in each of the eight intervals in Question 8, and give the name of the new interval—that is, name the enharmonic equivalents of the given intervals.

15. In what keys do the following intervals occur?

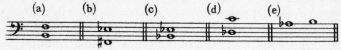

16. Name the intervals marked with a bracket in the following passage:—

17. (a) Write the notes giving the required intervals *above* the given notes;
(b) Write the notes giving the required intervals *below* the given notes:

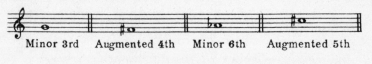

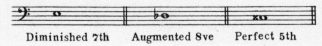

CHAPTER X

THE C CLEF – SHORT SCORE – OPEN SCORE – FULL SCORE – TRANSCRIPTION – TRANSPOSITION

167. Besides the G (treble) clef and the F (bass) clef there is another called the **C clef.**

Just as the treble clef fixes the position of the note G, and the bass clef fixes the position of the note F, so the C clef fixes the position of **middle C.**

The C clef however, has **two positions** (and formerly had more). It may indicate middle C as the *middle* line of the stave, thus:—

This is known as the **alto clef.**

Or it may indicate middle C as the line above, thus:—

This is known as the **tenor clef.**

168. The ALTO CLEF is in everyday use for the string instrument called the Viola. Formerly it was in common use for the Alto Voice, but not now. The student will be familiar with the look of a page of an anthem or part song showing four different voices on different staves.

Example (a) below shows former usage and also present-day *examination usage*, the C clef being used for alto and tenor parts.

Example (b) shows present-day usage: although the treble clef is used for the tenor voice, the music is sung an *octave lower*. Sometimes *two treble clefs* indicate the tenor line to remind the reader that the notes sound an octave lower.

Example (c) shows the universal method of stave arrangement for a string quartet (two violins, viola and cello).

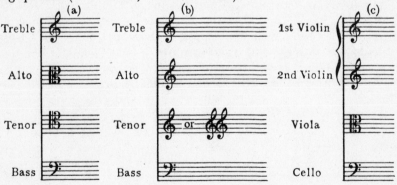

169. This allocation of one stave to each part is called **open score.**

When treble and alto share one stave, and tenor and bass the other, the arrangement is called **short score**—or **pianoforte score.** In pianoforte score the number of parts is constantly changing; there may be anything from one part to perhaps eight when both hands are playing big chords.

At (a) below we have *open score* for voices with each part singing middle C with the C clef for alto and tenor.

A (b) we have *open score* in present-day style, with each part singing middle C.

At (c) we have the same thing written as for a *string quartet*.

At (d) the four middle C's are shown as in *short score*.

In *piano score* there would be no need to use four stems—one middle C with one stem in treble or bass clef sufficing with perhaps a rest in the unoccupied stave (See " e ").

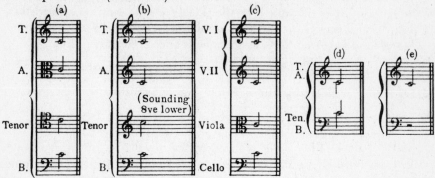

N.B.—The word " soprano " is frequently used instead of " treble "—hence the indication " S.A.T.B." (Soprano, Alto, Tenor, Bass).

170. Any arrangement of music with a separate stave for each voice or instrument (from 2 up to any number) is called *open score*.

Full score refers to open score on a large scale when many instruments (as in an orchestra) and/or voices are involved.

Orchestral score means open score for instruments only.

The open score shown at (a) and (b) in paragraph 169 is also called **vocal score** (viz. " score for voices "), but " vocal score " means also something different, as when we speak of the **vocal score of an opera or work for voices and instruments.** Here we refer to a score giving *the voice parts, and the accompaniment arranged for piano.*

In short score for voices the stems of treble (soprano) and tenor notes are always turned up, and the stems of alto and bass notes are always turned down.

The curly bracket joining the staves is also called a **brace.** It is customary to begin with a brace *and* a straight bar-line. In a string quartet or orchestral score first and second violins are bracketed together.

171. **The tenor clef,** although no longer used for voices, is still in use for tenor trombone, bassoon and cello parts when the music goes high.

172. The student may wonder why the C clef was thought necessary. The fact is that *it keeps the music on the stave*, and obviates the need for leger-lines.

Soprano music in the G clef rarely needs many leger-lines.
Bass music in the F clef rarely needs many leger-lines.
(that is, in vocal music)

But alto and tenor music written respectively in the G clef and F clef need many notes in " the no-man's land " of leger-lines.

Below are the normal compasses of alto and tenor voices:—

Here is an *alto* passage written in the *treble* clef:—

Here is the same *alto* passage written in the *alto* clef:—

Middle C →

(Note how the music is contained in the stave, without leger lines)

Here is a *tenor* passage written in the *bass* clef:—

Here is the same *tenor* passage written in the *tenor* clef:—

Middle C→

(Note once again the disappearance of all leger-lines but one)

173. The use of the C clef makes some re-arrangement of key signatures essential:—

    G Clef   Alto Clef   Tenor Clef

    G Clef   Alto Clef   Tenor Clef

Note that F sharp in the Tenor clef is placed below the C sharp.
The A sharp in the Alto clef may also be placed below the D sharp, in which case the contours of the signature at the same as in the Treble Clef:—

The pattern in flat signatures remains constant except that each flat moves to a different line or space to conform to the clef.

174. Re-writing—or transcribing—notes *at the same pitch* but with *different clefs* is a very common examination question: exercises in this process were given in Chapter I. These may be described as exercises in **transcription.**

Example (i)

Re-write (transcribe) this passage at the same pitch using the bass stave :—

Example (ii)

Transcribe this passage into the treble stave:—

Example (iii)

Re-write the treble passage in Example (i) above in the alto clef.

Method of Working

(i) It is important to remember the *position of middle C* in the alto clef:—

(ii) The first note in the given treble passage is G above middle C. Therefore write the key signature and fix this first note G in the alto clef, then the other notes fall into place:—

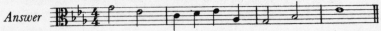

Example (iv)

Transcribe the bass passage in Example (ii) above into the Tenor clef.

Method of Working

(ii) The first note in the given tenor passage is F below middle C.

175. Examination questions may also ask for the re-writing of a passage an octave higher or lower. Such re-writing does not involve any change in the alphabetical pitch-names but generally involves a change of clef. This was also touched upon in Chapter I.

Example (i)

Re-write this passage an octave higher:—

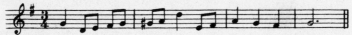

Method of Working

Clef, key and time signature are re-written, and the position of the first note fixed as the G an octave higher. It is then a simple matter to follow the rise and fall (contours) of the melody, taking care about the direction of the stems.

Answer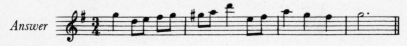

Example (ii)

Re-write the passage (Example i) an octave lower in the bass clef.

Method of Working

Bass clef key and time signatures are written and the position of the first note fixed. The note an octave below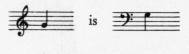

Answer

176. So far *no change of key* has been called for in re-writing musical passages, because either there has been no change of pitch or the music has been moved an octave higher or lower. If the melody has to be re-written at any interval distance other than an octave then a change of key has to be reckoned with, and the process becomes more complicated. Changing a passage from one key to another, the music remaining exactly the same but for the change in pitch, is known as **transposition.**

N.B.—Re-writing a melody at an octave higher or lower might be described as " transposition," but the term is generally understood to refer to a change of key.

177. Transpose this melody a tone up:—

Example

Method of Working

(a) The melody is in key F, and a tone above F is G. The new key signature will therefore be one sharp instead of one flat.

91

(b) When first trying this kind of exercise, it is helpful to write the two scales concerned:—

(c) The first   note of the transposed version will be B instead of A
The second note of the transposed version will be C instead of B flat
The fourth note of the transposed version will be D instead of C
The fifth   note of the transposed version will be G instead of F
The sixth   note of the transposed version will be A instead of G
The eighth note of the transposed version will be B instead of A
The *third* note of the given melody is B natural, which is really the subdominant sharpened.   The corresponding note in key G is C sharp, because the subdominant in key G is C a white note, whereas the subdominant in key F is a black note.
The *seventh* note of the given melody is the sharpened supertonic, which is G sharp, the supertonic itself being a white note.   As the supertonic A in key G is also a white note, the sharpened supertonic will be A sharp.
This completes consideration of the first bar.

Answer

Note that, wherever an accidental occurs in the given passage, it will be repeated as an accidental in the transposed version, but it does not necessarily follow that sharp will remain sharp, flat remain flat, or natural natural.
The next example in paragraph 178 should help to make this clearer.

178.   Transpose this melody down a diminished fourth:—
Example

Method of Working
(a) A diminished fourth below A flat is E natural
(b) The given melody is in A flat major: the transposed version will therefore be in E major.

Answer

Explanation of Accidentals
(1) *is the sharpened supertonic*
The supertonic in key A flat is B flat;
raised a semitone this becomes B natural.
The supertonic in key E is F sharp;
raised a semitone this becomes F double sharp.

92

(2) *is the sharpened subdominant*
    The subdominant in key A flat is D flat;
                  raised a semitone this becomes D natural.
    The subdominant in key E is A;
                  raised a semitone this becomes A sharp.

(3) *is the flattened leading note*
    The leading note in key A flat is G;
                  lowered a semitone this becomes G flat.
    The leading note in key E is D sharp;
                  lowered a semitone this becomes D natural.

(4) *is the flattened submediant*
    The submediant in key A flat is F;
                  lowered a semitone this becomes F flat.
    The submediant in key E is C sharp;
                  lowered a semitone this becomes C natural.

(5) *is the sharpened submediant* (See No. 4)
    The submediant in key A flat is F;
                  raised a semitone this becomes F sharp.
    The submediant in key E is C sharp;
                  raised a semitone this becomes C double sharp.
    It is necessary to *think oneself into the new key.*

179. It would have been quite wrong to treat the accidentals in paragraph 178 in the following manner:—

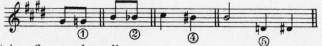

because (1) is a flattened mediant   —
                instead of the required sharpened supertonic.
    (2) is a flattened dominant   —
                instead of the required sharpened subdominant.
    (4) is a sharpened dominant   —
                instead of the required flattened submediant.
    (5) is a flattened leading note—
                instead of the required sharpened submediant.

180. Here is a more complex transposition—this time from F sharp major (six sharps) to D flat major (five flats)—viz., a transposition an augmented third down.

Example

Method of Working

(1) The first note is the tonic (F sharp). Write the new tonic (D flat) and put the other notes in their places *ignoring all accidentals* (the numbered notes):—

No. 1 will need sharpening: being a   flat   it will become a natural.
No. 2 will need flattening : being a' flat   it will become a double flat.
No. 3 will need sharpening: being a   flat   it will become a natural.
No. 4 will become the subdominant of the Scale—viz., G flat.
No. 5 will need flattening : being a natural it will become a flat.
No. 6 will need flattening : being a   flat   it will become a double flat.
No. 7 will need sharpening: being a   flat   it will become a natural.
No. 8 will need flattening : being a natural it will become a flat.
No. 9 will become the leading note of the Scale—viz., C natural.

Answer

Note: To try to transpose by laboriously considering each note separately and raising or lowering it by the required interval, is a misguided procedure. It is best to raise or lower the first note by the required interval, decide on the new tonic (*the first note is not necessarily the tonic*), find the new key signature, then *think in the new scale or key*.

181. Transposition from the G or F clef into one of the C clefs is one of the most difficult exercises in melody transposition.

Example

Transpose this melody a diminished fifth up into the tenor clef:—

Method of Working

(1) A diminished fifth above E is B flat ![notation]

(2) The first note is not the tonic: a glance at the last note will tell us that the tonic is C.

(3) A diminished fifth above C is G flat.

(4) Key G flat will have six flats.

(5) The first note is B flat below middle C, viz.: ![notation]

Answer

N.B.—An odd feature of these two versions—the one in C and the other in G flat—is that exactly the same positions on the staves are used in both cases. This is purely a coincidence. Notice the difference in some of the accidentals.

182. *Another Example*

Transpose this melody an augmented fourth down into the alto clef:—

Method of Working

(a) The key signature indicates A major or F sharp minor, but *the final note* establishes they key as A major.

(b) The first bar is intentionally misleading, B flat, F natural and D sharp being auxiliary or decorative notes not belonging to the key.

(c) An augmented fourth below A is E flat

(d) The new key signature will be that of E flat major. The first note in the given melody is the flattened supertonic of the scale of A, so that the first note of the transposed version will be the flattened supertonic of the scale of E flat, viz., F flat.

(e) The first note, F flat, of the transposed version is the F flat above middle C.

Answer

(1) Flattened supertonic.   (4) Sharpened submediant.
(2) Flattened submediant.   (5) Sharpened tonic.
(3) Sharpened subdominant.   (6) Sharpened subdominant.

183. Occasionally the interval distance for transposition is not named, the name of the new key being given instead.

Example

Transpose this melody up into the key of C sharp minor; using the alto clef:—

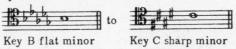

Method of Working

(a) The final note confirms the key as B flat minor.

(b) The first two notes are dominant F and tonic B flat.

(c) The corresponding notes in C sharp minor (four sharps) will be G sharp (dominant) and C sharp (tonic).

(d) The transposition will be from

Key B flat minor   to   Key C sharp minor

(e) Changing to the alto clef we have

C sharp minor

(f) The first note (G sharp) is below middle C.

Answer

QUESTIONS AND EXERCISES ON CHAPTER X

1. Why is the C clef so called? Show this clef on the stave indicating: (a) the alto voice; (b) the tenor voice.
2. For what instrumental purposes is the C clef used?
3. Explain: (a) open score; (b) short score; (c) orchestral score; (d) vocal score (two explanations of this).
4. (a) Write the signatures of the following keys in the alto clef:—
   B flat major, F minor, G flat major, C minor, D flat major, F sharp major.
   (b) Write the signatures of the following keys in the tenor clef:—
   E major, G sharp minor, G minor, B flat minor, F sharp minor.
5. (a) Re-write this passage an octave higher, retaining the treble clef:—

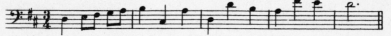

   (b) Transcribe it (same pitch) into the alto clef.
6. (a) Re-write this passage an octave lower, retaining the bass clef:—

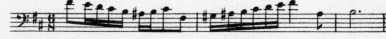

   (b) Transcribe it (same pitch) into the tenor clef.
7. (a) Re-write this passage in the treble clef at the same pitch:—

   (b) Re-write this passage in the bass clef at the same pitch:—

8. (a) Transpose this passage down a minor third, retaining the treble clef:—

   (b) Re-write the transposed version, using the alto clef.
9. (a) Transpose this passage up a major sixth, retaining the bass clef:—

   (b) Re-write the transposed version, using the tenor clef.

10. (a) Transpose this passage down a major second with no change of clef:—

   (b) Re-write the transposed version, using the alto clef.

11. (a) Transpose this passage up a diminished seventh with no change of clef:—

   (b) Re-write the transposed version, using the tenor clef.

12. (a) Transpose the given melody a tone down into the alto clef.
    (b) Transpose it a perfect fifth down into the tenor clef.

13. (a) Transpose the given melody a semitone up into the tenor clef.
    (b) Transpose it a diminished fifth up into the alto clef.

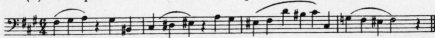

14. Transpose this alto passage down into the key of A flat major, using the tenor clef:—

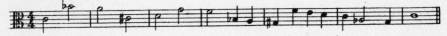

15. Transpose this tenor passage up into the key of D minor in the alto clef:—

CHAPTER XI

TRANSCRIPTION – TRANSPOSITION AND C CLEFS
(*Continued*)

184. Chapter X dealt with melodic transcription and transposition only. The same processes are now to be applied to passages in four parts—which may be an extract from a pianoforte piece, a string quartet or choral music in short score, or a simple hymn tune.

185. **Transcription of a passage in short score into open score with C clefs for alto and tenor.**

Example

Transcribe this passage into open score for S.A.T.B. using the proper clefs:—

Points to remember

(i) As each part will now have a line to itself the general rule about direction of stems will apply.

(ii) The start of the alto and tenor parts is all-important. Both alto and tenor parts begin with notes below middle C. Students often make the mistake of beginning these parts an octave too high or too low.

(iii) Since in the *alto* clef the middle line is middle C, whereas in the treble clef the middle line is B, it follows that all the notes in the *alto* clef will have alphabetical names one letter further on (*or higher*) than the corresponding name in the treble clef. The student, long used to the treble clef, must remember that:—

What was called B in the treble clef, is called C in the alto clef.
What was called C in the treble clef, is called D in the alto clef.
What was called D in the treble clef, is called E in the alto clef.
and so on.

(iv) Since in the *tenor* clef the fourth line up is middle C, whereas in the treble clef the fourth line up is D, it follows that all the notes in the *tenor* clef will have alphabetical names one letter *lower* (viz., preceding in the alphabet) than the corresponding name in the treble clef. The student must remember that:—

What was called D in the treble clef, is called C in the tenor clef.
What was called E in the treble clef, is called D in the tenor clef.
What was called F in the treble clef, is called E in the tenor clef.

186. Transposition of a passage in four-part harmony.

Example

Transpose the passage in paragraph 185 down an augmented second.

Method of Working

(i) This type of question is done in short score.

(ii) The key is B major, and an augmented second below B is A flat:—

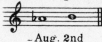

– Aug. 2nd

(iii) Write the signature of A flat major, and transpose the first chord. The soprano or treble note will be C (the mediant, corresponding to D sharp in the key of B major); the alto will be A flat (the tonic, corresponding to B in B major); the tenor will be E flat (the dominant, corresponding to F sharp in B major); and the bass will be the tonic A flat.

(iv) The first chord having been established each part may now be transposed in turn. It is essential to try *to think oneself into* the new key.

Answer

187. When a passage in short score is being transcribed into open score, it is necessary to exercise particular care in regard to any **crossing of the parts.** This occurs when treble goes below alto, alto above treble: tenor below bass, bass above tenor. Crossing of the parts is indicated in short score by the direction of the stems:—

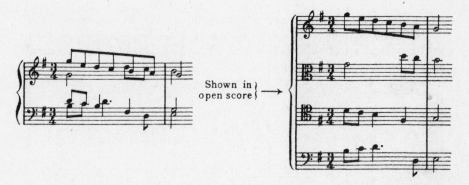

Shown in open score →

188.   When a passage in short score is to be transcribed into open score as for *string quartet*, it must be remembered that *only one part—the viola*—will need the C clef.   This part in a string quartet corresponds to the *tenor part* in vocal music, but the *alto clef* is used.   Both violins take the treble clef and the cello the bass clef. (See Example (c) in paragraph 168.)

189.   *Additional accidentals* may be required in open score.

At (a) below, in short score, the one accidental E natural in the alto applied also to the treble E following, as it is in the same bar and *on the same stave*.

At (b) below, in open score, the accidental E natural must be added to the treble, as the treble has a separate stave; otherwise E flat would be sung:—

190.   On the other hand *few accidentals* may be required in open score.

At (a) below, in short score, the treble E natural must be contradicted if the alto is to sing E flat, because both parts are in the same bar and on the same stave.

At (b) below, in open score, the alto would sing E flat without any special indication, because the parts have separate staves:—

One should think of the various voices (or instruments) as singing (or playing) their own parts *without being able to see the other parts* in open score.

100

191. The most complex type of question asks for **the transposition of a passage into another key combined with its transcription into open score with C clefs.** In such a case, after deciding on the new key signature and writing the clefs required, deal with the transposition and transcription of each part separately, remembering what has been said in paragraphs 187, 189 and 190 about accidentals and the crossing of parts.

QUESTIONS AND EXERCISES ON CHAPTER XI

1. Transpose this passage a major third down:—
    (a) retaining short score;
    (b) writing in open score as for a string quartet;
    (c) writing in open score as for voices with C clefs for alto and tenor

2. Transcribe this passage into short score:—

3. Transpose this hymn tune up into the key of B minor in open score with C clefs for alto and tenor:—

4. Transpose this passage up an augmented second, writing in open score as for string quartet:—

Andante

5. Transpose this passage a tone up, retaining pianoforte score:—

Allegro

CHAPTER XII

SIGNS – MARKS – ABBREVIATIONS

192. A **slur** is a curved line placed under or over a group of notes of different pitch indicating that they are to be performed *smoothly* (or, to use the Italian word, **legato**).

(In paragraphs 18 and 41 the **tie** or **bind** is described as a curved line joining *notes of the same pitch.*)

A slur is also used to indicate *phrasing*. To a singer a curve over or under a group of holes is an instruction to sing those notes *in one breath*. A singer marks the end of a phrase by *taking breath*: a pianist phrases by *raising the finger or hand* at the end of the curve or phrase mark:—

A slur also indicates the *bowing* of a string instrument. A violinist will play two or more notes grouped under one slur with one motion of the bow, that is, in the same direction, up or down.

The above passage from Beethoven's ' Minuet in G ' might be bowed thus:— Five motions of the bow

193. The Italian word of opposite meaning to *legato* (smooth) is **staccato** (detached). Staccato may be light and delicate or forcible and heavy, and is of *three kinds*:—

(a) Staccato as shown by dots over or under the notes, each note losing about one-half of its length in sound:

Played thus;-

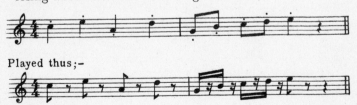

The custom of joining notes to indicate the beats should be noted; the joining of the semiquaver hooks in a straight line (even though the sounds are broken up by rests) greatly eases the work of the eye in reading.

(b) Staccato as shown by *dashes or daggers* over or under the notes, each note losing about three-quarters of its sound value:—

Played thus:—

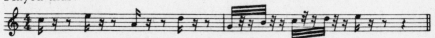

(c) Staccato as shown by *dots together with slurs or phrase marks*, each note losing only about one-quarter of its sound value:—

Played thus:—

194. (a) May be called *simple staccato* (short).
 (b) May be called *staccatissimo* (very short —" issimo " being the superlative).
 (c) May be called *mezzo staccato* (moderately short).
   A *single note* to be performed mezzo staccato is shown:—

195. A short horizontal line over or under a note indicates that the note must be given its full value—that is, held or sustained. The Italian term for *held* is **tenuto**; for *sustained* it is **sostenuto.** Some emphasis or stress is inevitable:—

196. In paragraph 95 the *triplet* is defined as a group of three notes played in the time of two of the same kind, the figure 3 being put over or under the three notes. A variant of the triplet involves the use of two notes of different length, also the inclusion of a rest as part of the triplet:—

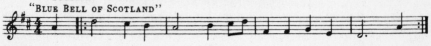

197. **Repeats** are indicated in several ways:—
 (a) By *enclosing the portion* to be repeated between double bar-lines, *placing two dots* after the first double bar-line and before the second. Four dots are sometimes used:—
"BLUE BELL OF SCOTLAND"

If the repetition goes right back to the beginning, one set of dots only need be used:—

But it is better always to use two sets and so avoid any uncertainty as to how far back one must go to repeat the passage.

(b) By enclosing the portion and placing dots as above but also writing *1st Time* (*Prima volta*) and *2nd Time* (*Seconda volta*) when there is a change in the continuation after the second time of playing:—

When repetition is made, the music under the 1st Time bracket is omitted and that under the 2nd Time bracket substituted.

Sometimes just " 1 " and " 2 " are written instead of " 1st Time " and " 2nd Time,"

(c) By the letters **D.C.** or the words **Da capo** (" from the beginning ") : this is a direction to the effect that a return must be made *to the first bar* of the music. **Da capo al fine** means " Return to the beginning and play as far as the word **fine** (the " end "). The word " fine " does not necessarily appear over the last bar of the printed music: the real end may be at the double bar-line about the middle of the printed music, thus:—

1st part of the music ‖ 2nd part of the music ‖

Real End   D.C. al fine
(" Fine ")

(d) By the letters **D.S.** or the words **Dal segno** (" from the sign ") a return being made only *to where the sign 𝄋 appears.*

(e) By the direction **bis** (French, through Latin, for " twice ") placed over a bar or a very short passage above a long square bracket or curve (slur). This direction is not much used now:—

(f) By certain signs such as / %. // in orchestral music indicating respectively the repetition of a whole bar or a group of notes. This method was designed to ease the work of the music copyist, and there is no reason to make use of it in printed music, which should always be clear, unambiguous and helpful to the sight reader:—

Generally speaking, the repetition of quavers is indicated by single lines, with two lines for semiquavers and three lines for demisemiquavers (corresponding to one hook for quavers, two hooks for semiquavers and three hooks for demisemiquavers). There is sometimes ambiguity in the type of abbreviation adopted for the repetition of a whole bar as in bar 2 of the above.

198. Abbreviations are used to indicate the repetition of a single alphabetical note.

(a) If a passage is to be played in quavers, then crotchets and minims with single strokes through their stems (derived from the single hook or tail of a quaver) would be a sufficient indication:—

(b) In the case of a semibreve, which has no stem, the stroke will be above or below the note:—

(c) If semiquavers are intended, *two* strokes will be drawn; if demisemiquavers are intended, three strokes will be drawn:—

(d) But if the original note is itself a quaver (which already possesses one hook) semiquavers would be indicated by one stroke, demisemiquavers by two, and so on:—

Notice that the quavers, semiquavers and demisemiquavers are grouped to show the (crotchet) beat divisions.

(e) In *compound time* (dotted note beats) the repetitions would be in multiples of 3:—

(f) *In simple time* the figure 3 or 6 with a dot after the note indicates that triplets or groups of six notes (sextuplets) are to be played in the time of the longer note:—

199. Abbreviations are also used to indicate *the rapid alternation of two notes of different pitch*—or the notes of a chord.

Once again the rapidity of the alternation corresponds to the number of strokes—one for quavers, two for semiquavers and three for demi-semiquavers.

The addition of the word **tremolo, tremolando** or the abbreviation **trem.** (" trembling ") signifies that there are to be as many alternations (or repetitions) as possible in the time value of the given notes—irrespective of the actual semiquaver or demisemiquaver indication.

(a) In the following example the notes C and E are to alternate as semiquavers in the time value of *one minim*. *Two minims* are written (however odd this may seem):—

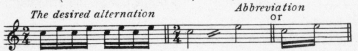

The second abbreviation is more usual. As minims are white or open notes, it is clear what is intended in spite of the notes being joined together as semiquavers. But crotchets could not be joined in this way, because their heads are black like semiquavers. Thus we could not use this abbreviation :—

and intend this effect ;-

This abbreviation would be essential ;-

(b) If the alternation of two notes is to continue for the duration of *one semibreve, two semibreves* are written and the appropriate line or lines added :—

Effect desired   *Abbreviation*

(c) If the time duration of the alternation is a crotchet, quaver or semiquaver, care is required to make this clear :—

To obtain   write   not

To obtain   write   not

(d)

Trem.

would be played

— if the tempo made it possible

(e)

In *pianoforte* music

Trem.

would be played   etc.

— as suitable to the idiom of the piano.

But in *orchestral string* music would be played ;-   etc.

— rapid movement of the bow across the strings.

200. When a note or rest is to be prolonged for an indefinite period, irrespective of time, the sign ⌢ or ⌣ (called **pause** or **fermata**) is placed over or under the note (or chord) or rest. The prolongation of the sound or rest is a matter for the performer to decide.

A pause of unusual length may be indicated by the abbreviation **L.P.** (**lunga pausa** or long pause).

G.P. (**Grosse** or general pause) is found in some orchestral scores— meaning a pause for the whole orchestra.

The pause sign may be found occasionally as a substitute for " fine " in music which makes use of the " da capo " indication, the pause marking the final bar.

201. The sign > indicating accent or stress has previously been mentioned in paragraph 19.

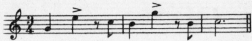

QUESTIONS AND EXERCISES ON CHAPTER XII

1. (a) What is a slur?
   (b) For what special purpose are slurs used in music for string instruments?
   (c) What is the difference between a slur and a tie or bind?

2. How many kinds of staccato are there and how do they differ from each other?

3. Write out the following passage as it would be performed according to the signs given:—

Andante

4. Rewrite the following passage, grouping the semiquavers into crotchet beats, and carrying the grouping-lines over the semiquaver rests where necessary:—

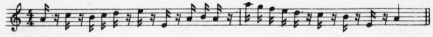

5. Write out the following in full as it would be played:—

6. Explain the abbreviations, D.C., D.S. and bis, with musical examples.

7. Write out the following in full as it would be played:—

bis

8. Write out the following in full:—

(a)

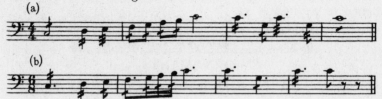

(b)

9. Write out the following in full:—

Moderato

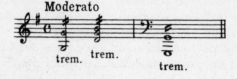

10. Write this passage as it would be played on the piano:—

Moderato

trem.   trem.

trem.

CHAPTER XIII

ORNAMENTS
(TURN – APPOGGIATURA – ACCIACCATURA – ARPEGGIO – MORDENT – SHAKE OR TRILL)

202. Ornaments in music (also called **grace notes** or by the French term **agréments**) are decorations or embellishments affecting the melodic line. Some are indicated by conventional signs or abbreviations; others appear as small notes or groups of small notes placed before the note to be decorated, this being known as the *principal note*. It is sometimes difficult to decide on the correct rendering of ornaments, especially in music of the seventeenth and eighteenth centuries. Modern composers prefer to write everything in full in notes of normal size, instead of entrusting the interpretation of signs and abbreviations to the performer's individual judgment. Knowledge of ornaments and their rendering is essential to the musician, hence the appearance of questions on ornaments in all examination papers in music.

203. The Turn

This ornament consists of four notes:—
- (i) the upper (auxiliary) note;
- (ii) the principal note;
- (iii) the lower (auxiliary) note;
- (iv) the principal note again.

The conventional sign for the turn is ∞

The sign may be placed either exactly *over* the principal note or *after* it.

The rendering of the turn is affected by:—
- (i) the length of the principal note;
- (ii) the position of the note;
- (iii) the pace or tempo of the music.

As with all ornaments (except the appoggiatura—which is described later) it should be played quickly, *and the slower the tempo the shorter the note values.*

204. **The Turn placed over the principal note**

If the pace is very quick and the principal note short, the turn may consist of four equal notes:—

Notice in the above example the use of the accidental to indicate that the lower auxiliary note is a *semitone* below the principal note.

Sometimes the turn consists of *five* notes, the principal note being sounded first, and three times in all. This usually occurs after a rest or a staccato note, or when it is desired to avoid altering the melodic contour by repeating notes that are not repeated in the unadorned melody:—

The second turn is delayed by a tie to correspond in time value to the first. If the second turn were of the normal four-note kind, the B first would need to be repeated.

There is no hard and fast rule as to when five note turns are required. An examination student would not be penalised through preference for the normal four-note type.

205. The Turn placed after the principal note

In this case the principal note is played first and held as long as possible, the actual turn being given the shortest possible notes. For *moderato* and faster tempi the turn should consist of semitones: for *andante* and slower, demisemiquavers should be used:—

When the turn is *between two notes of the same pitch*, the second of the two notes acts as the last note of the turn:—

112

206. **The Turn after a dotted note**

When the dot represents a fraction of a beat and is followed by a note completing that beat, then the *last note of the turn coincides with the dot*:—

The dot represents half the second (crotchet) beat, and the following quaver completes that second (crotchet) beat.

The middle example above might equally well be written:—

It is often a matter of individual taste whether a triplet turn is used without a tied note, or whether a group of four short notes, with the first of the group tied to the preceding-note, is preferred. The triplet turn without a tied note is easier to play, especially in a fast tempo.

Further examples of turns following dotted notes:—

207. **The Turn after a dot which does not represent a fraction of a beat**

The dot after a crotchet in $\frac{6}{8}$ time or after a minim in $\frac{6}{4}$ time does not represent a fraction of a beat, which beat is completed by the succeeding note—as in the examples in paragraph 206. In $\frac{6}{8}$ or $\frac{6}{4}$ time the dot following the crotchet or minim respectively completes the first half of the *main* beat. The rule given in paragraph 206 does not therefore apply:—

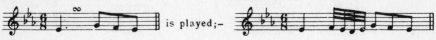

Nor does the rule apply when any dot is followed by *two* shorter notes to complete the beat:—

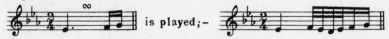 is played;—

208. The Inverted Turn

The sign is either ⌽ or ⌿ —the former being more common.

The order of notes in the inverted turn is: Lower (auxiliary) note, principal note, upper (auxiliary) note, principal note. It is used in exactly the same way as the turn, except that it starts with the *lower* note.

Adagio

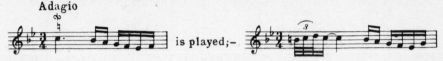 is played;—

The inverted turn is not anything like so commonly used as the other or *direct* turn. The notes required are more often written out as small notes. The example above from a Mozart sonata appears as follows:—

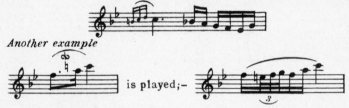

Another example

is played;—

209. The Appoggiatura (an Italian term pronounced approximately "ahp-podg-e-a-too-ra")

This is a small note (grace note) placed a step above or below the principal note. The word means "leaning," and the note leans to its principal note one step below or above, taking:—

(a) half the value of the principal note if undotted;
(b) two-thirds the value if dotted.

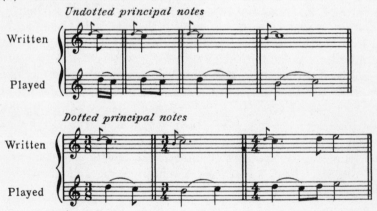

The auxiliary note takes the accent in every case.

Exception

In $\frac{6}{8}$ time the main dotted crotchet beats constitute duple time so that, when a bar contains one dotted minim and an appoggiatura, the treatment would be same as in $\frac{2}{4}$ time:—

210. Odd examples like the following, where the appoggiatura takes the whole value of the principal note, are occasionally met with:—

211. **An Appoggiatura before a chord**

An appoggiatura before a chord affects one note only of the chord; that is the one to which it is slurred:—

Modern practice is to write out exactly what is intended, and not to use the appoggiatura.

212. **The Acciaccatura** (an Italian term pronounced approximately " ah-tch-e-ak-a-too-ra ")

This is a small note written like the appoggiatura but with a stroke through it. Like that ornament it comes on the beat, but it is of the smallest possible duration, being " crushed " (the meaning of the word) into the principal note. Unlike the appoggiatura it need not be at the distance of a step above or below the principal note, any interval being possible, *and it is still in common use.* In writing out the actual effect of the ornament some facility in mathematical calculation is needed:—

Demisemiquavers should be used for moderate or fast speeds: and hemidemisemiquavers for slow speeds.

213. When the acciaccatura precedes long notes (minims and above) some difficulty is experienced in arranging the "played" version. The best procedure is to complete the value of a quaver first, then connect with a tie the other note-values required:—

This would be a
bad arrangement
for (d):—

214. **The Arpeggio** (Italian—"in the manner of a harp")

The sign ⟨ or (means that the notes of a chord are to be played one after the other (the lowest first), the sound of all the notes being sustained. Arpeggios are usually written out as demisemiquavers:—

116

215. The Arpeggio with Acciaccatura

The acciaccatura *is delayed to become the last but one note of the arpeggio*:—

216. The Mordent

This ornament consists of (according to usage in this country:—

(i) the principal note;
(ii) the note a tone above it (auxiliary note); } played as quickly as possible
(iii) the principal note again.

There is some confusion about the name. The German name for this ornament is the **pralltriller**, while the term " mordent " is reserved for the ornament which makes use of the auxiliary note a step *below* the principal note (this latter ornament being known in this country as the **inverted mordent**).

For examination purposes the terms **upper and lower mordents** would be accepted—or *direct* and *inverted*.

The sign for the *upper* mordent is ∿

The sign for the *lower* mordent is ∿

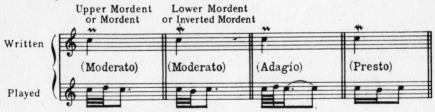

An accidental is frequently placed above or below the ornament:—

217. The Shake or Trill

This consists of the rapid alternation of the principal note and the note next above it—the sign being *tr*∿∿∿∿ (or *tr* alone). The sign is in constant use and saves immense labour in writing and expense in printing. The trill generally concludes with a *turn*. It may be long or short, the number of alternations depending on the pace of

117

the music (more being possible in a slow tempo) and the skill of the performer.

> If the tempo is *allegro or faster* the trill will generally be in semi-quavers.

> If the tempo is *allegretto or andante* the trill will generally be in demisemiquavers.

> If the tempo is *grave* (very slow) the trill will generally be in hemidemisemiquavers.

(a) *The shake or trill, unless otherwise indicated, begins with the principal note:*— *Written*

(b) *Its type of ending is indicated by two grace notes, and, as the shake must end on the principal note, an irregular note group will be the result:*—

Note that the type of note used for the small (grace) notes *does not determine* the type of note used for the trill. In the above example the grace notes are semiquavers, but the notes of the actual trill are demisemiquavers. The use of semiquaver grace notes is a convention. Sometimes these small notes are omitted: they are meant to be played just the same. Exceptions to this rule are mentioned below.

(c) *If it is intended that the trill shall begin with the upper note instead of the principal note, an acciaccatura is placed before the principal note. In such a case there will be no irregular note-group at the end:*—

(d) *In the next example the grace notes indicate that there will be no turn at the end of the trill:*—

(e) *When trills appear on short notes, fewer notes are naturally required:*—

The two trills are no more than two turns, each beginning with the principal note.

(f) *In the next example, there is no time for even a turn, and the trill is interpreted as a kind of mordent written in triplet fashion:*—

(g) *In the next example the trill amounts to a turn beginning on the principal note, being rather similar to* (e) *above:*—

(h) *If the notes at the end of a trill are printed as full-sized notes, they must be given their proper time-value:*—

(i) *A trill* **on a dotted note**, *with the principal note falling to the next principal note and anticipating it,* **stops on the dot** (*with no turn*) **the last note of the trill being equal to the time-value of the dot**:—

(j) *A trill over an interval or chord affects the top note only:*—

Two trill signs would be required for a double trill:—

(k) *Accidentals may participate in the shake. No natural would be needed in the following example to contradict the D flat in the abbreviation, but a natural would be needed when writing the ornamentation in full:*—

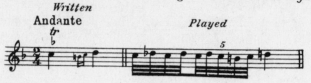

(l) *If grace notes precede a trill they are included in the time-value of the principal note and delay the beginning of the actual trill:*—

218. There are other signs for trills or shakes not now in use, and the student does not need to know them for examination purposes. As a matter of interest some of these old signs (to be met with for instance in the works of Bach and Handel) are given below:—

(a) The sign 𝔀 is a graphic representation of performance. In older music *the trill began with the upper (auxiliary) note:*—

(b) The sign 𝔀 indicated *a trill beginning with a turn:*—

(c) The sign 𝔀 indicated *a trill beginning with an inverted turn:*—

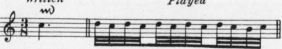

(d) The sign 𝔀 indicated *a trill ending with a turn (as in modern music):*—

(e) The sign 𝔀 indicated *a trill ending with an inverted turn:*—

219. All the ornaments listed so far are played in the time of the principal note: the appoggiatura and acciaccatura, although written immediately before the principal note, are not sounded before the time of impact of the principal note but coincide with it.

There is, however, a grace note (or sometimes more than one) which takes its time-value from the note which it follows. For this reason it is called an **after-note** or by the German name **Nachschlag**:—

(a) in the above extract from a nocturne by Chopin is an *after-note* taking its time from the preceding note. The other ornaments are of the orthodox kind, their time being taken out of the principal note that follows.

The after-note frequently partakes of the nature of an **anticipation-note** when it anticipates the sounding of the succeeding accented note:—

QUESTIONS AND EXERCISES ON CHAPTER XIII

1. Write the following passage in full as it would be played:—

2. Write this passage in full as it would be played:—

3. Write this bass passage in full as it would be played:—

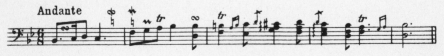

4. Write this passage in full as it would be played:—

Allegro moderato

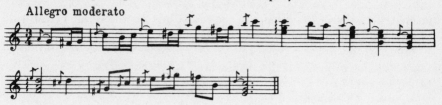

Treat the following passages similarly:—

5. **Presto**

6. **Lento**

7. Write this passage in two ways:—
   (i) as it would be played *adagio*;
   (ii) as it would be played *allegro*.

CHAPTER XIV

MUSICAL TERMS

220. Since the seventeenth century musical terms or directions regarding performance have been nearly all of Italian origin. Words of French and German origin are also occasionally used, while some composers use English directions. In the following lists French or German words are indicated by the abbreviations " Fr." or " Ger." There is room only for the most commonly used terms in a book of this size: for a comprehensive list recourse must be had to a dictionary of musical terms.

An approximation to the pronunciation of some Italian words is given in brackets.

A note on the varying pronunciation of certain consonants and vowels in combination will be found at the end of this chapter.

221. **Speed or Pace (Tempo**—Italian)
(Arranged in order from Slow to Fast)

Grave (grah-vay)—Very slow, solemn or serious.

Largo—Very slow and broad.

Larghètto—Slow and broad, but not so slow as *largo*.

Lento—Slow—but not so slow as *largo*.

Adagio—Slow.

Andante—(" Walking ") A somewhat slow tempo—" going " at an easy pace.

Andantino—An ambiguous term: it really means " less going," viz. " slower than *andante*," but is more often interpreted as meaning a little faster than *andante*.

Moderato—At a moderate pace—quicker than *andante*.

Allegrétto—Lively—moderately fast—quicker than *andante* but not so fast as *allegro*.

Allegro—Quick, lively and cheerful. (See also "*assai.*") In practice, movements marked " *allegro* " are not always lively and cheerful.

Vivace (Vee-vah-chay)—Lively.

Vivacissimo (-chee-see-mo)—Very lively.

Presto—Very fast—a degree of speed beyond *allegro*.

Prestissimo—As fast as possible—the quickest direction that can be given.

N.B.—**The Metronome** is a clockwork instrument which supplies the exact speed required by means of an inverted pendulum movement ticking each beat aloud. Assuming that the crotchet is the unit of measurement:—

Grave to *Lento*   might be ♩ = 40 to ♩ = 66
(The number indicates 40 or 66 ticks a minute)

Adagio to *Andante*   might be ♩ = 69 to ♩ = 84

Moderato to *Allegretto*   might be ♩ = 88 to ♩ = 108

Allegro to *Vivace*   might be ♩ = 112 to ♩ = 144

Presto to *Prestissimo* might be ♩ = 152 to ♩ = 208

Tempo commodo means at a convenient, easy pace.
Tempo ordinario means at a steady, ordinary pace.

222. Gradual Increase of Pace or Tempo

Accelerando (Atch-chel-er-ahn-do)—abbreviation: *Accel.*—Gradually increasing the speed.
Affretando—Hurrying, pressing on.
Calcando—Pressing on.
Incalzando (In-kahl-tsahn-do)—Increasing in speed and loudness—becoming more vehement.
Stringendo (Strin-jen-do)—Pressing on—hurrying.
Stretto—Pressed, drawn together—quickening the speed.
>   N.B.—This term has another meaning as applied to a fugue.

223. Gradual decrease of Pace or Tempo

Allargando—Broadening (enlarging) the tempo.
Calando—Decreasing in speed and tone (becoming both slower and softer).
Mancando—Dying away ⎫
Morendo—Dying away ⎬ Generally becoming
Perdendosi—Losing itself—dying away ⎭ slower and softer.
Rallentando (Rall.)—Slowing down ⎫
Ritardando (Ritard.)—Retarding ⎬ Becoming slower.
Ritenuto (Rit.)—Holding back ⎭
Slargando—Broadening the tempo (similar to *allargando*).
Slentando—Decreasing in speed.
Smorzando (being smothered or extinguished)—Fading away in tone and often in tempo.

224. Immediate increase of Tempo

Doppio movimento—Double the movement or speed, i.e. the music becomes twice as quick as the preceding.
Più (Pee-oo) *mosso*—More moved—quicker.
Poco più mosso—A little more moved—slightly quicker.
Veloce (Vel-o-chay)—Rapid, quick.

225. Immediate decrease of Tempo

Meno mosso—Less moved—slower.
Poco meno mosso—A little less moved—slightly slower.
>   N.B.—**L'istesso tempo**—In the same time
>   This term is used in conjunction with a change of time signature to indicate clearly the relation between the two signatures. It may bring about a *quicker effect* as when changing from $\frac{3}{4}$ to $\frac{9}{8}$. In such a case the new dotted crotchet pulse is the same as the previous undotted pulse, shown thus:—
>   𝅘𝅥. = 𝅘𝅥 *L'istesso tempo.*
>   Conversely a change from $\frac{9}{8}$ to $\frac{3}{4}$ may have a *slower effect*.
>   A change from $\frac{2}{4}$ to $\frac{3}{4}$, marked 𝅘𝅥 = 𝅘𝅥 *L'istesso tempo* preserves the same speed with a different recurrence of accent, and so on.

226. **Expression (Gradation of Tone: Loudness, Softness)**

Crescendo or *Cresc.* (Cre-shen-do)—Gradually increasing in tone, becoming louder. The sign ◁══════ has the same effect.

Decrescendo or *Decresc.*—Gradually decreasing in tone, becoming softer—the opposite of crescendo. The sign ══════▷ has the same effect.

Diminuendo or *Dim.*—Gradually diminishing the tone, becoming softer.

Dolce (Dol-chay)—Sweet, soft.

Estinto—(" Extinguished ") Barely audible—the extreme degree of pianissimo.

Forte (For-tay)—Loud and strong. Abbreviation *f*.

Fortissimo—Very loud. Abbreviation *ff*.

Forte piano—Loud, then with tone immediately decreased. Abbreviation *fp*.

Mezzo (Met-zo) *forte*—Moderately loud. Abbreviation *mf*.

Mezzo piano—Moderately soft. Abbreviation *mp*.

Piano—Soft. Abbreviation *p*.

Piano forte—Soft, then with tone immediately increased. Abbreviation *pf*.

Pianissimo—Very soft. Abbreviation *pp*.

Rinforzando—(" Reinforced ") Indicating an increased degree of tone or loudness. Abbreviation *rinf*.

Sforzando—Strongly emphasised—used for single notes or chords. Abbreviation *sfz* or *sf*.

Sforzando piano—Similar to forte piano but with more emphasis and contrast. Abbreviation *sfp*.

227. **Style**

Affetuoso—With emotion, affectionately, tenderly.

Agitato—Agitated, restless—at a quickening rate.

A piacere (Ah-pee-ah-che-ray)—At the pleasure of the performer as regards pace and style—the same as *ad libitum*.

Ad libitum or *ad lib.*—At the performer's liberty—the same as *a piacere*.

Animato—Animated, fast.

Appassionata—Impassioned, with strong emotion.

Aufschwung (Ger.)—Lofty, soaring.

Bravura—Boldness, brilliancy.

Brio—Spirit, fire, vivacity.

Burlando—Jesting or romping, comic.

Calmato—Calm, tranquil.

Calore—Warmth.

Cantabile (Kahn-tah-be-lay)—In a singing style (often applied to a pianoforte melody).

Cedez (Fr.)—Yield, relax the speed.

Einfach (Ger.)—Simple.

Espressivo or *Espress.*—With expression, expressive.

Fuoco (Foo-oh-co)—Fiery, dashing.

Furioso—Furious, wild, vehement.

Giusto (Jee-oo-sto)—Just, strict, exact; e.g. *Tempo giusto*, meaning strict or exact time.

Grazioso (Grah-tse-oh-so)—Graceful, elegant.
Giocoso (Jee-oh-koh-so)—Jocose, gay, merry.
Grandioso—Grand, lofty, pompous.

Impetuoso—Impetuous, vehement.

Leggiero (Led-ge-air-oh)—Light, nimble.
Lacrimoso—Tearful, sad.
Languido—Languid, faint.
Lusingando—Coaxing, caressing.

Maestoso (Mah-es-to-so)—Majestic, dignified.
Marcato—Marked, accented.
Martellato—(" Hammered ") An indication to play the notes forcefully and incisively.
Mesto—Sad, plaintive, melancholy.

Parlante or *Parlando*—(" Speaking ") This means that in singing the words must be declaimed, and in playing that a clear, crisp touch is required.
Patetico
Pathétique (Fr.) } Pathetic.
Pesante—Heavy, ponderous.
Piacevole (Pee-ah-che-voh-lay)—Pleasing, agreeable.
Piangendo
Piangevole } Plaintive, mourning, " weeping."
Pomposo—Majestic, dignified, pompous.
Portamento—Smooth—gliding from note to note—" carrying " the tone from one note to the next (particularly applicable to string instruments and the human voice).

Rasch (Ger.)—Quick, rapid.
Risoluto—Resolute, decided.
Rubato—(" Robbed ") In *Tempo rubato* certain notes are given more, others less, than their real value, i.e. some notes are " robbed " of some of their time which is given to others to heighten the desired effect or expression.

Scherzando (Sker-tsahn-doh)—Playful, light.
Sciolto (Shol-toh)—Free, nimble.
Secco
Sec (Fr.) } Dry, plain, unadorned.
Semplice (Sem-plee-chay)—Simple, unaffected.
Soave—Gently, softly, sweetly.
Strepitoso—Noisy, boisterous.

Teneramente—Tenderly.
Tranquillo—Tranquil, quiet.

Vigoroso—With vigor and energy.
Vivo (*Vif*—Fr.)—Brisk, lively.
Volante—Flying, light, swift.

228. Miscellaneous Terms and **Terms used in Conjunction with Others**

Al, All', Alla—To the; in the; at the; in the style of; like. e.g. *Alla marcia*—in the style of a march; *Da capo al fine*—(repeat) from the beginning to the ending.

Alt—Notes " in alt " are those contained in the treble octave beginning with and ascending from G above the clef.

A mezzo voce—With half the power of the voice.

Arco—A bow (of a string instrument).

Aria—An air, song or melody—a vocal solo with instrumental accompaniment in what is known as " ternary " or " A B A " form.

Assai—" Sufficient," but frequently interpreted as " very." e.g. *Allegro assai*—very fast.

Attacca—Begin the music which follows, without any pause or break. " Attack."

Ausdruck (Ger.)—Expression.

Ben—" Well," e.g. *Ben marcato*—well marked.

Bewegt (Ger.)—Moved, agitated, impassioned.

Capriccioso—Capricious, fanciful.

Cavatina—A simple aria without the second (middle) section or repetition (*da capo*).

Coda—(" Tail ") A finishing passage.

Col; coll'; colla; collo—" With the."
  e.g. *Col canto*—With the melody (a direction to the accompanist).
      Colla voce—With the voice (a direction to the accompanist).

Con—" With," e.g. *Con moto*—With movement.
      Con bravura—With boldness and brilliancy.
      Con brio—With fire and spirit.

Destra—Right, e.g. *Mano destra* (abbr. M.D.)—The right hand.
      Main droite (Fr.) (abbr. M.D.)—The right hand.

Di—By; of; from; with, etc. e.g. *Tempo di Valse*—Valse Time or Waltz Time.

En dehors (Fr.)—Prominent: a direction to bring out a certain tune or part.

Etwas (Ger.)—Rather, somewhat; e.g. *Etwas langsam*—Rather slow.

Gruppetto—The Italian word for the ornament called a turn.

Inhalt (Ger.)—Contents (Index of a volume).

Klein (Ger.)—Small.

Ma—" But," e.g. *Allegro ma non troppo*—Quick but not too much so.

Maggiore (Mah-jee-o-ray)—Major.

Mit (Ger.)—" With."

Molto—Much, very, extremely; e.g. *Molto adagio*—Very slow.

Sinistra—Left; e.g. *Mano sinistra* (abbr. M.S.)—The left hand.

Tre corde—Three strings; an indication to release the left pedal on a piano (see *una corda*).

Un; Un'; Una—One; e.g. *Una volta*—Once (one time).

Una corda—One string; an indication to use the left pedal on a piano. The hammers (on a grand piano) are then moved so that one string only is hit instead of three.

Un poco—A little.

Voce (Vo-chay)—Voice; e.g. *Sotto voce*—Under voice, in an undertone.

Vorspiel (Ger.)—Prelude.

Zart (Ger.)—Soft, delicate, tender.

229. Names of the Notes in English, Italian, French & German

English	Italian	French	German
C	Do	Ut or Do	C
C sharp	Do diesis	Ut dièse	Cis
C flat	Do bemolle	Ut bémol	Ces
D	Re	Ré	D
D sharp	Re diesis	Ré dièse	Dis
D flat	Re bemolle	Re bémol	Des
E	Mi	Mi	E
E sharp	Mi diesis	Mi dièse	Eis
E flat	Mi bemolle	Mi bémol	Es
F	Fa	Fa	F
F sharp	Fa diesis	Fa dièse	Fis
F flat	Fa bemolle	Fa bémol	Fes
G	Sol	Sol	G
G sharp	Sol diesis	Sol dièse	Gis
G flat	Sol bemolle	Sol bémol	Ges
A	La	La	A
A sharp	La diesis	La dièse	Ais
A flat	La bemolle	La bémol	As
B	Si	Si	**H**
B sharp	Si diesis	Si dièse	**His**
B flat	Si bemolle	Si bémol	**B**

230. Major and Minor in English, Italian, French and German

English	Italian	French	German
Major	Maggiore	Majeur	Dur
Minor	Minore	Mineur	Moll

231. Italian Pronunciation

Italian pronunciation follows the spelling very closely and all syllables are sounded separately.

a is pronounced as " ah "—as in *adagio*, and never like the English " a " as in *lake*.

c before " a," " o " and " u " is pronounced like " k "—as in *poco*.

c before " e " and " i " is pronounced like " ch "—as in *dolce*.

cc before " a," " o " and " u " is pronounced like " k-k "—as in *attacca*.

cc before " e " and " i " is pronounced like " t-ch "—as in *accelerando* and *capriccioso*.

ch	before " e " and " i " is pronounced like " k "—as in *scherzando*.
g	before " a," " o " and " u " is hard—as in *lusingando*.
g	before " e " and " i " is pronounced like " j "—as in *giusto* and *giocoso*.
gg	before " e " and " i " is pronounced like " j "—as in *maggiore*.
i	is pronounced " ee "—as in *andantino*.
qu	is pronounced " kw "—as in *tranquillo*.
sc	before " e " and " i " is pronounced like " sh "—as in *crescendo* and *sciolto*.
u	is pronounced " oo "—as in *una corda*.
zz	is pronounced either " d-dz " or " t-ts "—the latter as in *mezzo*.

INDEX

References are to paragraphs unless otherwise stated

131